YITHI LABA

DIARIES OF THE ROLE OF ZAPU-ZPRA WOMEN COMBATANTS IN THE LIBERATION STRUGGLE OF ZIMBABWE
VOLUME 1

METHEMBE HILLARY HADEBE

INGWALADI
PUBLISHERS

YITHI LABA

DIARIES OF THE ROLE OF ZAPU-ZPRA WOMEN COMBATANTS IN THE LIBERATION STRUGGLE OF ZIMBABWE
VOLUME 1

YITHI LABA:
DIARIES OF THE ROLE OF ZAPU-ZPRA WOMEN COMBATANTS IN THE LIBERATION STRUGGLE OF ZIMBABWE.
Volume 1

ISBN 978-1-77921-134-7
EAN 9781779211347

INGWALADI PUBLISHERS

15211 Nkulumane 12
P O Box Nkulumane
Bulawayo.

YITHI LABA:
DIARIES OF THE ROLE OF ZAPU-ZPRA WOMEN COMBATANTS IN THE
LIBERATION STRUGGLE OF ZIMBABWE.
Volume 1

First publication: 2022
Designed and typeset by Mthokozisi Moyo
Copyright INGWALADI PUBLISHERS 2022

Cover picture:

Chief of Staff Ambrose Mutinhiri emphasizing a point to Mkushi Camp women combatants during a parade. accessed from Zenzo Nkobi Collection kept at Mafela Trust and South African History Archive (SAHA).

INGWALADI
PUBLISHERS

ACKNOWLEDGEMENTS

It is difficult for me to retrace the whole history of compilation and writing of this book due to its prolonged gestation. I wish to extend my sincere gratitude to the late Director of Mafela Trust, Zephaniah Nkomo, who was behind me in all the research endeavors that culminated in this book. He helped me to identify participants in this study and generously shared with me knowledge and photographs of Zimbabwe People's Revolutionary Army (ZPRA) women combatants. Through his efforts, I could access information from the institutional repository, which would have been difficult without his help. Sadly, he did not live long enough to see this work. Equally, I wish to thank the late Stanley Elish Gagisa Nleya who also helped me in understanding the type of military training that was received by both men and women combatants. His insight made it possible for one to understand the experiences of the women combatants as they narrated their recruitment phase, training lifestyle, and their subsequent deployment. I also extend my gratitude to the late Jane Lungile Ngwenya, who shortly before her passing on, shared the context of women nationalists and combatants in ZAPU-ZPRA, now that most of recruits looked up to her as the pioneer among women with the ranks of ZAPU. Indeed, we are poorer with the passing on of these three freedom fighters!

My indebtedness would be incomplete without mentioning the extraordinary efforts that were demonstrated by various ZPRA freedom fighters through the compilation of this book. I wish to name, particularly, Abel Mazinyane, Baster Magwizi, Stanford Moyo, Billy Mzamo, Marshal Mpofu, Charles Makhuya, and McCloud Tshawe who acted as content editors in giving accurate names of other cadres and in providing useful information on the subject matter.

It is, however, necessary to mention and acknowledge, above all, the interviewees who availed their time to document their experiences and roles. Quite frankly, it was not an easy task as the interviews invoked traumatizing memories leading to anger and shedding of tears. I appreciate their continued bravery in coming out to tell their experiences that were a missing puzzle in the history of the nation. From these experiences, the nation will appreciate selfless sacrifices that were made to liberate Zimbabwe from the clutches of colonialism. Their collaboration in this project proved invaluable to me throughout the formulation and revision of this book.

This book would be a much weaker piece without the rigorous editorial comments, and critical inputs from Professors Jocelyn Alexander, JoAnn McGregor, and Dr. Terence M. Mashingaidze. They all availed their time, carefully read and edited the series of transcribed interviews while proffering useful suggestions throughout all stages. I also wish to thank Alexander and McGregor for the generous grant that made it possible for one to reach out to various interviewees and institutions for data collection and subsequent printing and production of the book. This publication also acknowledges in a special way the use of some selected pictures accessed from the Zenzo Nkobi Collections stored at Mafela Trust and the South African Historical Archives (SAHA).

I must not forget to appreciate the help I got from Mthokozisi Moyo, Nokholo Matshazi, Johannes Mpofu, Sindiso Bhebhe, Justice Sibanda, and CnC production who critiqued the work and helped in the fine-tuning of this publication. Finally, I am profoundly indebted to my parents, family, my wife, and son. I extend my gratitude to you as you understood the pressure I underwent. The unconditional support eased pain ascribed to data collection and book compilation.

CONTENTS

PICTURES AND ILLUSTRATIONS

ZPRA CAMPS AND AN OFFICE IN ZAMBIA

Fig 1: Shows distribution of ZPRA camps and an office in Zambia.

The map legend:

1. Freedom Camp
2. Zimbabwe House (Lusaka)
3. Nampundwe Camp
4. Kafuwe Camp
5. Victory Camp
6. Solwezi Camps
7. Mkushi Camp
8. Mwembeshi Camp

ZPRA CAMPS AND AN OFFICE IN ZAMBIA

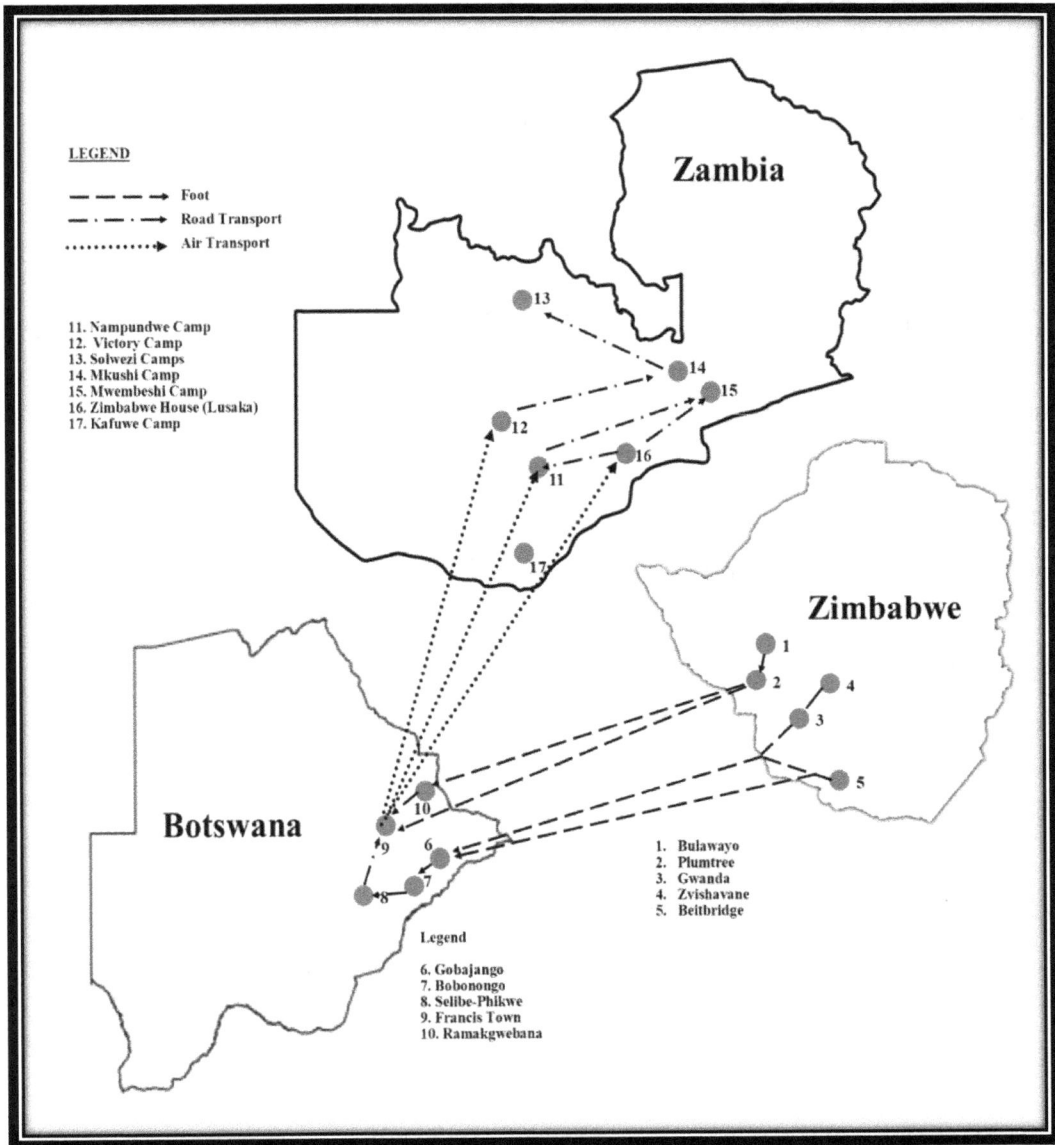

LEGEND

- — — → Foot
- — · — · → Road Transport
- · · · · · · · → Air Transport

11. Nampundwe Camp
12. Victory Camp
13. Solwezi Camps
14. Mkushi Camp
15. Mwembeshi Camp
16. Zimbabwe House (Lusaka)
17. Kafuwe Camp

Zambia

Zimbabwe

Botswana

1. Bulawayo
2. Plumtree
3. Gwanda
4. Zvishavane
5. Beitbridge

Legend

6. Gobajango
7. Bobonongo
8. Selibe-Phikwe
9. Francis Town
10. Ramakgwebana

Fig 2: Shows the travelling and transition routes followed by ZPRA recruits from Zimbabwe to Zambia via Botswana.

ABBREVIATIONS AND ACRONYMS

AAPSO	Afro-Asian Peoples' Solidarity Organization
ANC	African National Congress
DDR	Disarmament, Demobilization and Reintegration
FC	Freedom Camp
LMG-Choir	Light Machine Gun-Choir
NDP	National Democratic Party
NSO	National Security Organization
RF	Rhodesian Forces
SRANC	Southern Rhodesian African National Congress
USSR	Union of Soviet Socialist Republics
VC	Victory Camp
ZANLA	Zimbabwe African National Liberation Army
ZANU	Zimbabwe African National Union
ZAPU	Zimbabwe African People's Union
ZAWU	Zimbabwe African Women's Union
ZIPA	Zimbabwe People's Army
ZNA	Zimbabwe National Army
ZPRA	Zimbabwe People's Revolutionary Army

CHRONOLOGY OF EVENTS FOR FEMALE COMBATANTS' TRAINING

1975 March:	First group of 9 ZPRA female combatants is recruited and trained as part of a group of 800 combatants at Mwembeshi.
1976 January:	ZIPA formed in an attempt to unite ZPRA and ZANLA fighting forces.
1976 January:	The group of 800 combatants is moved to Mgagao (including nine female combatants) for joint training with ZANLA under the then newly formed ZIPA.
June 1976:	Mgagao crisis. ZPRA forces together with their 9 female combatants are attacked by the Chinese and ZANLA cadres at Mgagao.
1976 June:	The group of 800 combatants is forced to move from Mgagao to Morogoro with the 9 female combatants.
September 1976:	The second group of ZPRA female combatants, are recruited and trained as part of a group of 2 000 mostly male combatants at Mwembeshi.
March 1977:	The third group of female recruits is selected from Victory Camp to receive military training at Mkushi Camp. The group includes those that were recruited from Manama Secondary School. It is estimated that the number of the trained was around 1 200.
October 1978:	Bombardment, hundreds of Zimbabwean refugees are massacred by Rhodesian Forces at Freedom Camp in Zambia.
October 1978:	Hundreds of female recruits and their female instructors are massacred by the Rhodesian Forces at Mkushi Camp in Zambia.
October 1978:	Survivors at Mkushi are taken to Solwezi Camp.
November 1979:	Lancaster House Conference reaches a constitutional settlement to end the war.
February 1980:	ZANU wins British-supervised elections. Independence of Zimbabwe and Robert Gabriel Mugabe becomes the Prime Minister.

GLOSSARY OF TERMS

Assembly points: these were established as meeting points to facilitate the demobilization of thousands of freedom fighters deployed throughout the country. Freedom fighters were given a specific time frame to gather at these points after the cease-fire came into effect. The idea was to ensure that freedom fighters registered their names, surrendered their weapons and had serial numbers of their weapons recorded.

Bombardment: a continuous attack with bombs, shells, or other missiles.

Big Bhawa: a large house that accommodated recruits at Victory Camp.

Ceasefire: an agreement to stop fighting a war for some time so that a permanent agreement can be made to end the war.

Comrade: a fellow soldier or member of the guerrilla armed forces. In this publication participants argue that at Victory Camp they also used the term comrade to refer to lice. Lice was a dominant feature at the camp.

Further military training: an advanced form of training where an accomplished military officer is deployed or assigned after completing a standard military training at entry-level.

Guerrilla: a member of a small independent group taking part in irregular fighting, typically against larger regular forces.

Guerrilla warfare: is a form of irregular warfare in which small groups of combatants, such as paramilitary personnel, or irregulars, use military tactics including ambushes, sabotage, raids, petty warfare, hit-and-run tactics, and mobility, to fight a larger and less-mobile traditional military.

Member of the high command: an influential ZPRA officer with a rank endowed with the authority to make and take far-reaching military decisions within the rank and file.

Instructor: accomplished military personnel recognized as skilled enough in their profession to teach and impart military skills to recruits and soldiers. These military instructors brought their invaluable experience and knowledge to the learning process.

Military recruitment: the activity of attracting people to, and selecting them for military training, deployment, and employment.

Operation: refers to an action of attack, onrush, onset or onslaught.

Reconnaissance: military observation of a region to locate an enemy or ascertain strategic features and information gathering to be used in various military strategies for recruitment, operations, and deployment.

Refugee: a person who has been forced to leave their country to escape war, persecution, or natural disaster.

Refugee camp: a temporary settlement built to receive refugees and people in refugee-like situations. Refugee camps usually accommodate displaced people who have fled their home country, but camps are also made for internally displaced people.

Rice: Apart from it being known as food by many, the term rice was used widely at Victory camp to refer to the Russian combat uniform that was worn at the camp. The uniform had small fine lines that resembled the grains of a rice. The combat was later named after its design.

FROM THE SENIOR VETERAN'S DESK

This publication comes out at a time when the state is finally engaged in programs of reconstructing the history of the liberation struggle through street naming exercises and rejuvenating institutions tasked with the mandate of documenting the liberation memories. It is in this epoch that the history and contribution of Zimbabwe African People's Union (ZAPU) and her military wing Zimbabwe People's Revolutionary Army (ZPRA) are now recognized and appreciated after years of being sidelined and omitted in the state memory. Therefore, this book provides a missing link in the research area of ZPRA's contribution during the liberation struggle and further bridges the silence or gaps existing of the role of ZPRA's women combatants during the liberation struggle.

It presents a sound testimony of Zimbabwe People's Revolutionary Army (ZPRA) women combatants' selfless contribution in various forms and at different levels to the attainment of the independence of Zimbabwe. These unsung heroines occupied different roles with ease and worked hard in achieving all assignments in their respective departments to which they were assigned and deployed. Had it not been for their unconditional efforts and contribution, it is possible the liberation struggle of Zimbabwe could have dragged on much longer than it took.

This is an eye-opener, not only to the local freedom fighters but to the entire population and the world over, that spells out the determination, effort, and zeal of women combatants to achieve whatever challenge they were faced with. It shows their powers, prowess, and equality to males without any prejudice. Their liberation story finally proves that war efforts were not a monopoly or a preserve of males but a collective effort by all in realizing independence for all. *Yithi laba* spotlights key issues for critical analysis in contemporary Zimbabwe that while women combatants were fighting hard to liberate the country, they also fought for their recognition, empowerment, and more fundamentally, women's rights. Many today see women's rights as a post-colonial entity not knowing that these were also a defining value in the liberation struggle.

The benefit from this book should transcend vertically and laterally. Written in a more accessible language, the book should be used for academic purposes at schools, colleges, and universities as a teaching instruction, further research purposes, and infusing the testimonies of women combatants into the school syllabi. It can also be used by government institutions and policymakers to inform policy directions to advance programs for liberation history that include but are not limited to street naming exercises, roll call, and the establishment of memorials where ZPRA women combatants should also feature.

Finally, I plead and demand that women combatants' efforts be honored accordingly by the state while they are still alive by equipping history researchers with resources to document the rich contribution of women and men and, more importantly, the state should honor women combatants, by looking at their welfare and returning the contributions which they made.

Mr. Marshal Mhambi Mpofu.

INTRODUCTION

This book is an exploration of the underexplored war experiences and the participation that was demonstrated by Zimbabwe People's Revolutionary Army (ZPRA) women combatants during the liberation struggle of Zimbabwe. Formally recruited from 1975, these heroines trained at Mgagao, Morogoro, Mwembeshi, Mkushi and Solwezi. They later received further advanced military training in various overseas countries. This enabled them to occupy different roles and positions within the revolutionary party and its military wing. These roles and assignments ranged from deployment as security personnel, intelligence officers, and military instructors; in the administration department some were posted in the typing and secretarial pool; on diplomatic missions, and in the civil humanitarian service as nurses and teachers. Henceforth, in this book, women combatants claim their space in the liberation historiography, which has never been fairly accorded to them owing to their systematic omission in the state memory particularly, in street naming exercises, school curricula, and academic scrutiny. To say the least, most historical studies in Zimbabwe have remained androcentric with very little attempt to explore the subject matter of ZPRA's women combatants.

The title of this publication, *Yithi laba* in the Ndebele indigenous language is taken from one of the songs that were sung by Light Machine Gun Choir (affectionately known as the *LMG Choir*) in various ZAPU-ZPRA camps. The song narrates a story of ZPRA guerrillas who were recruited, trained, labelled by the colonial regime as 'terrorists' and disappeared from their native land for a while, and only appeared and emerged gloriously upon gaining independence. In this regard, the title carries with it the same reasoning alluded to by the song that ZPRA women combatants existed and played a pivotal role during the liberation struggle, but at a later stage found themselves ostracized, forgotten and absent in the historiography of the nation. In this publication, ZPRA women combatants reclaim their space in the historiography of the nation and illustrate various contributions they undertook to dislodge the colonial regime based on unfiltered self-narrations.

The *Yithi laba* title spotlights a key critical issue of plurality as opposed to individualism. This indicates that the liberation struggle was not a one-man band nor was it won out of an individual effort. It was through the selfless and combined efforts of everyone in the party structure and rank-and-file in unity with the masses. This is illustrated through their experiences of fighting the regime in a coordinated and united front thereby depicting a clearer war strategy of us versus them!

A few studies that have attempted to discuss the role and participation of ZPRA women combatants have tended to discuss the participation of women nationalists in ZAPU, or those linked with the male nationalists thereby overshadowing the experiences and roles of trained combatants. Women combatants indeed paid homage to the ZAPU women nationalists as they drew inspiration from them, especially Jane Lungile Ngwenya. Many participants in this publication agree that she inspired them to join the liberation struggle owing to her broadcasts, which they heard at home in Zimbabwe. Her interview has been included in this publication to provide a context of how women were accommodated in the party, now that she was a pioneer female nationalist who worked with other male nationalists. Owing to her radio broadcasts, women combatants maintain that Ngwenya was the greatest recruiter through her radio program that became a vehicle for indoctrinating and inviting the masses into the liberation struggle.

However, while Jane occupied an influential position in the party, she did not receive military training like other female nationalists such as Ruth Chinamano, Theresa Thaka, and Thenjiwe Lesabe, among others. There is always that temptation of discussing the contribution of ZAPU female nationalists to provide the entire liberation story and submerge the voices of ZPRA women combatants. There was a distinction between party members and trained combatants. Women nationalists were members of the party and had roles that they played, while women combatants were recruits of the military wing and later accomplished soldiers. These should be treated separately.

More often than not, the role and contribution of ZPRA women combatants have always been told from the perspective of Zimbabwe African National Liberation Army (ZANLA's) women combatants. This is to say, there is an assumption that the contribution of ZANLA women combatants was also what ZPRA women combatants did thereby giving a misleading and narrow narrative about the latter. These two military wings had a different strategy of training and deploying their trained women combatants and hence some roles and wartime contributions differ. For example, women combatants from ZANLA were deployed in the front with their male counterparts but ZPRA did not deploy its women combatants to the front.

To rectify these errors about the role and participation of ZPRA's women combatants and to reconstruct their war-time-participation in the liberation struggle, this book assembles these women's wartime stories of how they were recruited from their homes and how they participated and contributed to the liberation struggle in various episodes together with their male counterparts. Based on self-narration and presented in a biographic style, women combatants in this publication narrate the course of their lives from the point where they were recruited, their lifestyles at the camps, training, deployment, and finally end their stories at 1980 while locating their role and contribution.

One interesting fact is that while going through the chapters, one will discover that some of these combatants contributed immensely before receiving military training. Their role and contribution did not begin after receiving military training. Rather, the training positioned them to directly deliver and participate in ZPRA's war effort. Within their narrations, they tell stories of their lived experiences and situate their stories in a manner in which each one saw and experienced. This explains why some were able to detail certain scenarios whereas others would prefer to narrate the same scenario differently. Each had a unique experience.

Informed by the first recruitment of ZPRA women combatants from 1975, this publication is confined to the period from 1975 to 1980 for various reasons. The year 1975 marked a turning point in the history of ZPRA as nine women combatants got recruited and received military training. Only two of the nine pioneers have been included in this publication. These are Grace Muchachi and Bvundzai Tawona. They later became military instructors not only to other women recruits but also to men. Before 1975 there was an attempt to train and recruit women combatants but such did not see the light of day as it is held that ZPRA was not yet ready to train women combatants. Instead, those who had wanted to be trained combatants were sent on scholarships to study abroad. These include Julia Masangweni, Cecelia Nkomazana, and Martha Chimaya, among others.

Between 1975 and 1980, there was an influx of recruits as three new groups of women got recruited and trained at Morogoro, Mwembeshi, and Mkushi at the height of various operations. The most well-known episode of recruitment was the Manama group where a large number of students were taken from school to join the liberation struggle. In tracing the contribution and the role of women combatants, the period under review presents various activities that were carried out by women in different units of deployment. By extension, the period recorded major bombardments at Freedom Camp, Mkushi and also covers the Mgagao crisis. In all those setbacks, women combatants were present as discussed in the chapters. This publication hoped to go beyond 1980 in an effort to understand the captivating role of combatants and, how they adapted back into the society in the post-colonial state. This was however not possible for reasons discussed below.

As highlighted before, trained ZPRA women combatants were never deployed to the front. There are more questions than answers as to why, after investing so much in the recruitment and training of women the military wing was still hesitant to deploy them to the front. The interviewees narrate that they were not officially told why they were not deployed to the front and as such, this decision remains a mystery. However, there are many cited reasons as to why women combatants were not deployed to the front, which range from the fact that their numbers were smaller as compared to their male counterparts and that the military wing decided they could not deploy men and women together as means to safeguard women against exploitation. This line of thinking suggests that possible issues of indiscipline and exploitation were to arise between combatants and soldiers could end up pursuing agendas contrary to the ethos of the war. Others have also suggested that the reasons for not deploying women could be attributed to time factor: had the war further prolonged, it is possible that women were going to be deployed. Such discussions have been raised by women combatants within the publication.

From these interviews, it is clear that the formal instruction was that women should train and take up responsibilities at the rear. Here, they took up various assignments with the reasoning that in those positions or assignments, they were safer and were able to discharge their duties while their male counterparts fought hard at the front to liberate the zones where they were deployed. From\ testimonies, it is clear that women sacrificed and contributed a lot during the liberation struggle. However, others still felt that some type of jobs they did were less essential as they wanted to go to the front as promised by Jane Ngwenya. It is Jane Ngwenya who had promised them that when they finally accomplished their training, it was then that they would be deployed to the front. Poignantly, it never turned out the way they had anticipated.

Participants in this publication preferred to narrate their contributions and experiences of the liberation war up to Demobilization Demilitarization and Re-integration (DDR). Their preference was not surprising, as they were not prepared to discuss their post-colonial experiences granted that there was civil strife known as *Gukurahundi* where they were also affected directly or indirectly as former ZPRA forces. The popular view by participants was that the post-colonial experience is very sensitive and might weigh down and shift the focus of the intended objective of documenting their role and contribution during the armed struggle.

The other conspicuous area which women combatants preferred not to discuss was the issue of relationships, sexuality, and cases of rape. Regarding relationships, three interviewees noted that relationships existed. One of them, in particular, narrates how she fell pregnant on the eve of independence and was withdrawn from the department where she was deployed and sent to Victory Camp where she was accommodated with other women who were pregnant. It is from these three interviewees that one understands that the training and the entire liberation struggle did not hold everything at constant. Relationships existed and ZAPU-ZPRA had a strategy of accommodating and regulating them. One certain fact is that relationships were not confined among recruits or within trained personnel but it was an issue that cut across the liberation movement and army, where those in authority used power dynamics to establish relationships. This explains why some women combatants got married to high-profile ZPRA cadres as some of these relationships date back to the days at the training camps.

Of importance to note, none of the women combatants spoke about issues of menstruation, sexual harassment, and rape. After probing, interviewees avoided such subject matter and rather focused on their contributions and roles that they undertook during the liberation struggle. There are two fundamental reasons why they decided to silence menstrual, sexual harassment, and rape issues. The fact that women combatants were interviewed by myself, a male far removed from their generation, made it difficult for them to share stories of such a nature. This is where indigenous African philosophy came into play where elders (in this case women combatants) do not discuss sexuality issues, especially with young men. The second aspect that one noted, is the fact that women combatants were not forthcoming in discussing sexual harassment and issues of rape as some of the perpetrators are still alive and, in some respects, they are powerful individuals, endowed with authority in the society. Therefore, discussing their unpleasant history might have attracted victimization and retribution towards interviewees.

Interviewees were identified diversely. A number of them were identified and contacted through the institutional database from Mafela Trust, and ZPRA Veterans Trust. These organizations were able to identify women combatants who had been in various training camps. Others, who are not affiliated under these different ZPRA institutions, were identified using the snowball technique in which those that had been identified earlier using the institutional database were able to refer the researcher to reach out to them in different places.

As a researcher, one had to travel long distances to conduct interviews with them. Such interviews were recorded using an audio or video recorder so that the footage is later transcribed into text. Two of the interviewees in this publication were interviewed online through a virtual platform as they reside overseas. It is those transcribed footages that have been converted into chapters in this publication. Interviewee questions were deliberately omitted from the chapters and slightly edited the transcripts themselves for ease of reading. The meaning of the text has not been changed.

During the interviewing process, some ZPRA women veterans would burst into tears while narrating the experiences they went through during the war while others would request deferment and resume the interview after minutes, hours, or days. This was a common occurrence, especially among survivors of the Mkushi bombardment and those that still have sad personal experiences that invoke trauma. The suffering involved in telling these stories was considered worth it in order to place this history on record. In this publication, they have, however, faced such experiences with fortitude in narrating their contributions to the liberation struggle. These experiences had remained largely unheard. This publication extensively relied on interviewees and some personal collections on the subject matter from participants. This publication also uses and acknowledges photographs from Zenzo Nkobi collections accessed from SAHA online.

The approach in this book is such that readers go through the chapters, which are made up of individual interviews, to understand each one's experience. Experiences were different depending on each woman's background, where they trained, and, more importantly, to which department they were deployed. In some instances, one might feel as if there is a repetition of information when going through the chapters. It is in that context that one needs to understand that the liberation struggle was not a single event but a process and hence participants diversely saw similar or different events depending on what they were going through at the time. This is explained by how chapters are packaged to show coherence, invoke emotions and break the monotony in reading a similar plot altogether by including illustrations, and photographs among other things.

Within this broad parameter of the story of ZPRA's women combatants, two other women are included in this publication, although they were not trained women combatants. This has been done to holistically understand the dynamics of women combatants within the phase of recruitment up to the training. Maretha Dube narrates how she was withdrawn by her parents after she had successfully crossed with the Manama group of students to Botswana. Her story represents all those that were withdrawn from the war and she maintains that they had their fair share of the role that they played back home, now that they were exposed to the guerrilla activities and the objectives of waging the liberation war against the Smith regime.

Going through the book, some interviewees narrated that a point of difficulty came when they were in Botswana where the colonial regime had organized outreach for parents to withdraw their children who had been recruited to join the struggle. Those who were successful to train as combatants refused to be withdrawn despite pressure from their parents or had already been flown to Zambia by the time of the otreach.

One surviving member of the Light Machine Gun (LMG) Choir, Happiness Sibanda, has been included in this publication. Her interview seeks to radically debunk the widely held notion or assumption that women were mere singers in the liberation struggle. Of course, women sang in the liberation struggle but not women combatants. For ZPRA, singing was done by a specialized unit called LMG to preach the ideology of the party and its army, provide hope to the combatants and the entire population at home. LMG operated within ZPRA's camps in Zambia and not back home in Zimbabwe. Her interview provides context for the formation of the LMG not in a combatant training camp but a refugee camp and shows that the choir worked with the commissariat department in preaching the ideology of the party and her military wing.

It is important to note that a few high-ranking ZPRA male counterparts have been included in this publication for two fundamental reasons. First, war was generally regarded as a male domain and preserve by ZAPU and hence ZPRA had trained male combatants long before the recruitment of women combatants. It was male cadres who recruited, selected, trained, and deployed women combatants, hence the need to understand how they blended and trained with female combatants. Furthermore, the story of women and men combatants would be incomplete without the other. Hence this publication radically departs from creating fiction or rather an impression that women combatants operated in isolation yet, in fact, there was collaboration.

Using different individual experiences that have been brought together, chapters touch on hot issues of the liberation landscape, how women combatants were recruited, the horrors of traveling up to the point of training, and unraveling controversial matters that others might find sensitive, thereby raising more questions than answers. Although it is not absolute, this book strives to provide a missing link and bridges the silence or gaps in the literature about ZPRA's women combatants, especially about their contribution. The aim is to bring varying perspectives to the fore, open debate, and stimulate critical analysis about the contribution of ZPRA's women combatants. The book hopes to provide the nation with a deeper appreciation of the immense contribution women combatants executed during the struggle after years of absence within the historiography.

Mr. Methembe Hillary Hadebe.

CHAPTER 1

'We pioneered the first-ever training of women combatants in ZPRA'

Grace Muchachi
(Mwembeshi, Mgagao, and Morogoro trained cadre)

Fig 3: Freedom Fighter, Grace Muchachi, who was part of the first group of nine female combatants to be trained with men at Mwembeshi, Mgagao, and Morogoro. She survived the Mgagao attack. After training, she was a military instructor in various ZPRA camps. She also worked at the ZPRA Headquarters in Lusaka called Zimbabwe House. In 1980 she was integrated into the police auxiliary force.

My name is Ethel Noko. I was given Grace Muchachi as my war name. I was born in Gwanda at a place called Halisupi to the Kwete Noko family. I am the fourth of six children two of whom are boys. It is unfortunate that one of my elder brothers died during the liberation war.

I joined the war of liberation in the year 1975 at the age of 15. It all started when we heard stories of Joshua Nkomo and the liberation struggle. We could hear our parents complaining of white people demanding cheap labour and taking all of their arable lands. Parents said they were forced to surrender all their livestock through taxes and also made to dig trenches[1]. Our parents were complaining that white people were disrespecting them, discriminating against them, not allowing them to practice their culture, customs, and traditions. They argued that they were treated like slaves who were not allowed to complain but comply.

In the area where I come from, it [was] very easy to go and cross the river over to Botswana. We used to see people passing and crossing over to Botswana in groups of two or three. The war had started and at around 10 to 11 years of age I decided to join the struggle. I was seated with my uncle who was around eighty years of age. While we were seated, from the blue he said to me, '*Bayahamba abafana kanti lina lihlaleleni abanye behamba?*' (Other kids are joining the struggle to fight against the regime, why are you not joining them?)

I internalized his words and became determined to join the struggle. Our churches started to encourage the youth to join the struggle. This influenced me and other youths to join the struggle.

On one evening during youth choir practice and prayers we decided to join the struggle. At the end of it all, four managed to go and others deserted at the last minute. Among those who managed to go was my nephew Wonder (Moffat) Ngulube, my sister-in-law, her young brother and I.

We managed to cross over to Botswana, people asked us where we were going and in response, we said we were attending a big church conference. It was not as easy as you might think. After we had crossed over to Botswana, the two boys began to dig for information on how we could join the war under ZPRA as recruits in Zambia.

In Botswana, we arrived at my aunt's place and lived a normal life cooking, fetching water and firewood while the boys also did some duties at home. While doing our house chores, boys continued digging for information on what they would do for them to be recruited to Zambia. They sought this information at stores in Gobajango.

They used to frequent the stores at Gobajango to get more information on the process of recruitment. At the shops they would enquire on how people or rather youngsters who would want to join the struggle and cross to Zambia go about it. They would go there to understand whether there was a way in which those who want to join the struggle would be recruited and have their names noted. The person who they approached told them to write their names down and wait for the response. A guy called Motsumi took down their names. Wonder submitted names of all four if us.

After capturing our names, the person told them to wait as they will eventually

---

[1] In 1951 there was construction of contour ridges and grassed waterways under the compulsory Native Land Husbandry Act (NLHA). Contour ridges were associated with oppression during the colonial era in Zimbabwe, which many saw as forced labor.

communicate with their superiors that there are youth who want to join the struggle. The person instructed my brothers to wait for the day when they will be taken by vehicles to a safe place as recruits. They were told to wait for details of the date of recruitment and departure to the venue in Botswana.

In about two to three days, my relatives, an uncle and cousin called Theodophala, who had come from South Africa where they were working as migrants in gold mines of Witwatersrand Native Labour Association (WNLA) arrived in Botswana. They had come from South Africa with intention of seeing my aunt and proceeding to Zimbabwe. We told them it was no longer possible to go back to Zimbabwe as the war had started. We told them that we were forced to go out of the country to join the struggle. They were convinced and decided to join us.

The day finally came when the vehicle to ferry us arrived. The eight of us left to join the struggle. The vehicle carried us from Gobajango, took us to Bobonong. We were told to stay in Bobonong and we complied. [After a] day an instruction was sent to the recruiting personnel and a car took us to Selibe-Phikwe prison. It was already evening when we arrived at Selibe-Phikwe and a cell had been prepared for us to sleep in as a group.

The next morning, we were taken to the main Selibe-Phikwe prison where we stayed for several days while they were still working out logistics on how we would be moved. The recruitment officers were also waiting for the info from their superiors. Before we reached Zambia, we were taken from Selibe-Phikwe to Francistown. When we reached Francistown, we were then divided. Girls were taken to a house that had representatives of ZAPU. There were two men, one called Black Swine and another called Normal. There was also a guy called Matthew Makoni.

We had left the boys but they later came over as Francistown became the transit centre. While we were at a ZAPU house where the four of stayed, five girls and three children from Beitbridge joined us. One of them was called Bvundzai Tawona[2]. We stayed in that house from July to December.

In December we were later flown by aeroplane to Nampundwe camp in Zambia. Nine of us were the first group of girls to reach Zambia and receive military training. This was the first [women's] group on ZAPU's side and there are some who had gone there [after] working at the party. One girl defaulted to ZANU as a result of the differences between ZANU and ZAPU during the joint program. [Due to] differences between ZAPU and ZANU, the Zambian government decided to remove and relocate ZANU to Mozambique, and Zambia was left for ZAPU. Only one girl called Jane Ndlovu who came from Gokwe refused to join ZANU and remained with ZAPU. She was later made to join us. This is the Jane

---

[2] Bvundzai Tawona was among the first group of nine female combatants to receive ZPRA's military training. Refer to her full interview which is also included in this publication, page 10.

that we trained with[3].

As the only nine females recruited, we were combined with other male recruits known as the group of 800. One early morning in Nampundwe we were taken through a registration process conducted for them to understand and know who exactly they had recruited. This is the time I was given the war name Grace Muchachi. Up to now people know me as Grace because that was the name I was given at war and I came back after the war and registered a birth certificate as Grace Ethel Noko. Were given war names to protect our identity for security reasons. It was also done to protect our families back home. In the event the enemy identified our names it would be difficult to trace and locate our families back home.

The next morning, I went for exercises and toyi-toying before attending lessons. This remained one of the daily routines. The first lesson that all recruits were taught was commissariat. It was important as it reminded each one of us of the reasons why we had joined the struggle. We were taught ZAPU policies, vision, and mandate. It also instilled discipline, and taught recruits how to behave and encouraged respect as ZPRA soldiers. The emphasis in the commissariat lessons was for us to understand why we had left Zimbabwe to join the struggle. ZAPU emphasized that regardless of race we are all humans, and therefore we are all equal. We were taught to fight discrimination: the manner in which the whites treated blacks as second-class citizens. There was need to fight the colonial system, to be free and to free every Zimbabwean citizen until whites understood that they were in Africa and Zimbabwe [is] a land of black ancestry.

As nine girls [we] were accommodated inside Zambian military barracks a few meters away from the 800 group. Despite separation, we remained in the same camp. After exercises, toyi-toying, and lessons we went back to the camp to sleep.

The emphasis of the commissariat lessons was for one to understand why they had left Zimbabwe to join the struggle. This was because ZAPU emphasized that whether you are black or white we are all people or humans with rights to equality. We were taught that the waged struggle was not on the basis of race but we were fighting a system that saw black people as perpetual minors, second-class citizens, and people that have no rights. The party emphasized that there were a lot of good whites who understood the concept of the struggle.

There was a need to fight the colonial system to be free and free every Zimbabwean citizen. It gave us the strength not to be afraid and to fight the

---

[3]Her real name was Ratidzo Ndlovu and she came from Gokwe in Midlands Province. She was among the first group of nine female combatants who trained at Mwembeshi, Mgagao and Morogoro. Upon completing her military training, she became a military instructor to other female combatants at Mwembeshi and was later redeployed at Mkushi camp. However, she is said to have died during the bombing at Mkushi on the 28th of October 1978.

enemy. To stand firm and fight. It also made us eager to fight as the lessons made it clear that it was now the time to fight. In mid-January, we were moved to Mwembeshi as authorities felt that Nampundwe was too close to Lusaka town and it was a transit camp. Nampundwe had no training facilities necessary to prepare recruits for war.

Mwembeshi was about 200kms away from Lusaka towards Zambezi towards the inland. We were taken to Mwembeshi and ZPRA had already sent out some of its senior officers who had trained before us. These received us and prepared us to be trained. These included senior instructors like Stanley Elish Gagisa Nleya, Khwela, Jack Mpofu, Philip Valerio Sibanda, and Eddie Mlotshwa-Sigoge among others[4].

A day after arrival we woke up early to sort out the logistics of how we would live and train. We resumed the early exercises, toyi-toyi, and long runs of 4 to 5kms depending on the instructor's program. As girls, we were never given special training, we were trained like our male counterparts. While we were still at Mwembeshi, Nkomo came and requested his command structure to remove girls and assign us to go back to school as he felt that the training was not appropriate for us but more appropriate for males. He requested that we be removed from the camp and sent back to school. We refused to go back to school and wanted to remain under military training. He tried to negotiate with us but we still insisted that we wanted to remain as soldiers. He went back and sent Dabengwa to convince us to go back to school.

Dabengwa also insisted that the training was meant for [men and] and not us as it required resilience, but we still insisted that we wanted to remain as soldiers. He understood and went back. Am sure he told them that we wanted to become soldiers. The training started, we would go for exercises, then go to breakfast, proceed to parade, and eventually allocated different assignments. For example, some would be assigned to the kitchen to cook, others attend military lessons, some do gun assembly and tactics, physic, etc. This was done on a rotational basis which meant that within a week, one would have covered all of what was taught during that week.

After that, we would then dismiss go to lunch as companies. Our instructors were very firm, professional and well-mannered. They knew how to discipline and advance command. In spite of their goodness towards us, if you claimed not to be feeling well, they would still make you take part in drills and trainings. Afterwards they would jokingly tease you saying the sickness has disappeared.

Sometimes a few of us would not get a plate of food because the cooks may have

---

[4]Cited cadres were ZPRA's senior military instructors who trained men and female combatants at various levels and stage of the liberation struggle. They further went for various operations in the front at the height of the liberation struggle.

underestimated the quantities. Despite that, instructors would request us to return to the training and lessons and encourage you to wait for the next meal. This taught us to ensure that food quantities are shared fairly.

When we [were] still training at Mwembeshi for about three months, they formed Zimbabwe People's Army (ZIPA) which was a joint training for ZPRA and ZANLA. This was after the recommendation from other regional parties to have the two military wings unite and fight the enemy as a joint force [rather] than divided. They formed ZIPA, which in turn affected our training in Mwembeshi as everyone was supposed to be part of it. Including us the female recruits.

I was then taken to Mgagao together with [the] other eight female recruits. When we arrived at Mgagao, it was surprising that we were the only females from ZPRA - the nine of us. It took time for the joint program at Mgagao to be finalized because of the ideological differences. We went for close to a month without proper training. Without ZANLA, ZPRA continued morning exercises, *toyi-toyi*, and concentrated on gun drills but this time we used sticks. After that we usually went to eat our daily meals in the kitchen. The schedule was modelled to as that of Mwembeshi. I should emphasize that we were not doing such together with ZANLA but alone as ZPRA.

When we arrived at Mgagao, we found Chinese who were meant to train us, however, conflict ensued and the trainings failed. The Mgagao conflict/crisis emanated from the kitchen. ZANLA and ZPRA would alternate to cook in the kitchen and we would arrive for meals in a particular order. For example, we arrived in companies within our military wings. ZPRA had companies A, B, C, sections, and platoons.

On this particular day ZANLA cadres were on duty to cook for everyone. The first ZIPRA company to go to the kitchen did not find any food. ZANLA told them that there was no food for them. ZPRA began to bemoan what ZANLA cadres had done asking why they were denied food. They complained about why on that day ZANLA was denying them food. While this was happening, I was on my way to the kitchen with a group of girls.

To the surprise of many, ZANLA reacted violently. ZANLA went ahead and called a backup of Chinese instructors who came with guns. As I was coming from the tent with other females, we heard gunshots and saw people running. We couldn't see what was going on we joined the running lot. We then realized that our cadres were under attack.

There was a boy who was part of us during the training. I remembered his face from Francistown. He was younger than me, and he was called *Mapheka-pheka*. When we were running away, we heard ZANLA cadres who were attacking us calling him saying, '*Mapheka-pheka dzoka*' (*Mapheka-pheka* come back). This made us wonder, why he [Maphekapheka] was being called by name in the midst of the crisis! This is what brings one to the realisation that within ZIPA there were more differences than similarities.

While running away from ZANLA attacks, we heard them saying, '*Vakadzi musarove, batai chete*' (Do not attack girls, just block them and bring them back). We don't know what was their intention for us, I mean the female recruits. Your guess is good as mine. We refused to return and continued to run with other ZPRA members. We ran with all our might. Stanley Elish Gagisa Nleya, who was our senior instructor, ran ahead and positioned himself in front of us to instruct and command. He instructed us to save ourselves, I remember he gave commands of where we needed to crawl, run, stand, etc. It is through his bravery and commands that most of us survived and managed to sail through. That training from Mwembeshi helped all of us on physical fitness and adhering to the command while sharpening our physic.

The attack on us started at 1pm [or] noon, this stretched up to midnight and others were still running to join us at the front. Some were moving seeking places to hide while endeavouring to move forward. This was still at night. Some managed to join us after the guns ceased a bit. We began to look for the main road although the instruction from Stanley Gagisa Nleya was that when we heard sounds, we should quickly return to the bush and hide as we did not know whether the sounds were from our enemy or our cadres. We did all those things through the command and signals from the instructors. We finally made it to the main road to regroup. We followed the main road to the police station called Iringa where we put up for almost two days while waiting for others and also waiting for a decision from the command structure on logistics and the way forward.

Female cadres did not arrive in Iringa at the same time. I remember others came after a day or so. We had been worried about what could have happened to them. Others died, I remember one male I knew from Gwanda called Mlobi Moyo, died there.

When we were still at Iringa, after an assessment and other considerations, Tanzania decided to send us to Morogoro. The party then agreed to us [going] there away from ZANLA as it was evident that the ZIPA issue was not working at all. The party had recommended that we discontinure training at both Mwembeshi and Mgagao. Normally, training lasted six months but we only trained three months at Mwembeshi. We failed to have meaningful training at Mgagao under ZIPA.

Morogoro was chosen as a running base as it had already trained a lot of ZPRA cadres. We went to Morogoro and got trained there. This is where we interacted with real guns as part of our training. Grouped according to our companies, we shared AK47s because they were not enough for all of us. We would also assemble and attend land mines lessons. This was the routine training at Morogoro. Notable instructors who took charge of the training in Morogoro included Rodwell Nyika, Dry Phetsheya, Mike Reynolds, Madodo, Sam Fakazi and Tshile Dubhu Nleya.

After the training at Morogoro, while we were waiting for a pass out, Bvundzai and I were taken back to Mwembeshi, Zambia, to become instructors of females whose group was dubbed 53. The command decided that we go back to Zambia to train new female recruits but under the watch of our main male instructors. This was also a strategy to use us as examples to motivate recruits that it was possible to have female cadres. We then became instructors.

I was there with the girls for about four months and I was later transferred to Victory Camp (VC) to do a similar assignment. While at VC, I was assigned for further training in Cuba. I was not going alone; but with other male and few female cadres. Members of 53 that had arrived in Mwembeshi were also selected to train in Cuba. In total, twenty of us comprising of eight girls and twelve boys went to Cuba. I remember Hazel, Zegeu, Isabel, and Lydia Mbayiwa.

In Cuba we underwent the same military training but with lessons of National Security Organization (N.S.O) on how to penetrate and establish structures with civilians within the liberation war. These were preparatory lessons on how one would carry themselves while dealing with civilians in urban and rural towns. While I didn't carry out the N.S.O lessons in Zimbabwe, it was a study on how one would operate in towns with the civilians. Others did it in Zimbabwe.

Upon return from Cuba, I was deployed to Zambia party headquarters at Zimbabwe House in Lusaka. I worked there under the administration section which was led by John Nkomo. I became instrumental in managing office work, scheduling the programs of high-ranking officials for international conferences. I was not integrated into the army but in police as an auxiliary force.

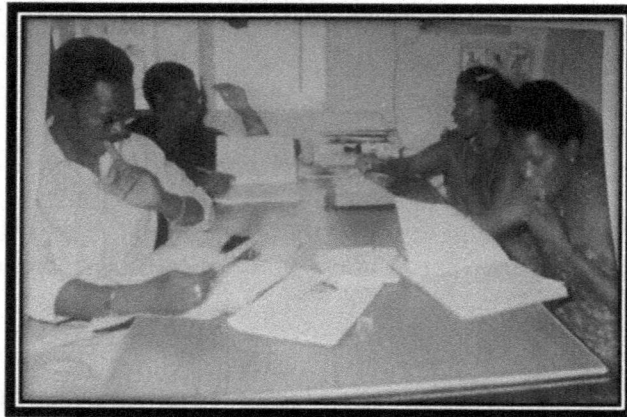

Fig 4: Mapeni in white shirt (immediate left), Grace Muchachi (far left near the window), Hazel Ndlovu in read dress (immediate right) and an unidentified colleagues at Zimbabwe House in Lusaka. **Picture source**: Accessed from Grace's personal archive.

Fig 5: (Left side picture): Jane Ndlovu on the far left and Audrey on the right side. There were among the first group of nine women combatants to be trained with Grace and Bvundzai at Morogoro.

CHAPTER 2

'I still do not regret why I joined the liberation struggle'

Bvundzai Tawona
(Mwembeshi, Mgagao, and Morogoro trained cadre)

Fig 6: Freedom Fighter, Bvundzai Tawona, who was one of the first group of nine women to be trained with men at Mwembeshi, Mgagao, and Morogoro. She survived the Mgagao attack. After the training she was a military instructor in various ZPRA camps.

My name is Thoriso Moyo and my war name was Bvundzai Tawona. I went to war in 1975, when I was still in grade five. I was very young by then. I went with my sisters and other girls from the community to free our country Zimbabwe from the colonial yoke.

Then, I was at Shashi primary school in Beitbridge. I am originally from Beitbridge from the Chawu-chawu village where my father was the village head and my maternal grandfather was the local chief of the area. My mother was also a staunch activist against the colonial regime. One time when we went to school, soldiers from the Rhodesian Défense Forces approached the school authorities instructing them to draw up a list of all boys and girls who had reached an age where they could join the war. Rumour had it that the drawn list were people who were meant to be killed to minimize the possibility of recruitments by Joshua Nkomo and his boys.

When we got home my mother told us to go and join the war. The most painful part is that I was the last born in my family and I was afraid to go and join the struggle. My mother insisted that even if I remained at home, I was going to be killed if they search and find my sisters and me at home. Considering what our parents used to tell us about brutality and issues of discrimination at work we convinced each other there was a need to join the war.

My parents would talk about Joshua Nkomo and position him as a leader chosen to free Zimbabwe from colonial chains. I was too young to know Joshua Nkomo. On our way to bed our mother reiterated that we needed to go and join the war so that we save our lives. There were looming rumours that the Smith regime was about to come and capture every boy and girl of my age and above.

My father had a radio that was constantly tuned into news and current affairs. Coincidentally, a program was broadcast on the radio where we heard Jane Ngwenya inviting children to join the struggle. I may not quote her directly but she said something like,

'Wozani, lizokulwa likhulule ilizwe lenu. Wena ohleziyo uhlaleleni uthi umbhobho wakho uzathwalwa ngubani. Woza uzokulwa ukhulule ilizwe lenu? (Come along and join the liberation struggle. Am directing this message to you who is listening. Who do you think will carry your gun? Come to the struggle to free your country Zimbabwe)

She was one of the first women to join the struggle in Zambia, she spoke over the radio[5]. The way Jane dramatized her program was as if she was watching her audience. All these things culminated in inspiring us to join the struggle more determined than before. It was easy to get the impression that we could go and receive our guns upon arrival in Zambia and start shooting settlers.

I was among the first group of nine girls to train as military cadres. But other women had gone before us and worked tirelessly for the party. These included Jane Ngwenya, and many others that I no longer remember. These were active in forming Zimbabwe African Women's Union (ZAWU)[6]. I also remember Mrs. Thaka whom we also found in Zambia.

Let me come back to the central theme of my journey to Zambia. We were taken by vehicles from Selibe-Phikwe to Francistown where we joined other four girls,

---

[5]Ms. Jane Ngwenya was a ZAPU broadcaster based at Lusaka in Zambia. Her program was widely heard inside Zimbabwe and many ZPRA veterans both female and male combatants say they got inspired by her to join the struggle, owing to her broadcasts they heard at home in Zimbabwe. Her full profile and interview have been included in this publication.

[6]Named female nationalists were active in coordinating the programs of ZAPU-ZPRA under the women's league called Zimbabwe African Women's Union.

among them was Grace Muchachi[7]. We found them staying at ZAPU House. In December of the same year, we were taken to Zambia by air to a place called Nampundwe camp. Nine of us were the first group of girls to receive military training and reach Zambia. This was the first group on ZAPU's side and apart from some who had gone ahead of us to work for the party.

I have to emphasize that those who were the first female recruits to receive military training were only nine of us. Recruitment was very different. As I have narrated, for us, it came from our different contexts because our parents had seen that the Rhodesian force was now in full throttle looking for at least mature children likely to join the struggle. We got recruited as a pre-emptive mechanism of preventing the purging of able-bodied youths.

Some other groups of female recruits who came after us had a different version of how they were recruited. Others tell they were recruited at school, particularly those from Manama who were recruited by ZPRA cadres. By then, we were now instructors teaching other females, girls, how to fight while in Zambia, Mwembeshi camp. I should also state that we trained both males and females.

Another type of recruitment was conducted by guerrillas deployed from Zambia to Zimbabwe. Such kind of recruitment occurred during the course of fighting whereby they interacted with civilians. When I went to the war our group comprised of nine people. I was with the four Beitbridge groups and the other four we found in Francistown, the group that had Grace Muchachi. We found another girl in Zambia, her name was called Jane, not the senior Jane Lungile Ngwenya. Namely, there was Bvundzai, Grace, Belinda, Constance, Jane, Audrey, Gladys, Alice, Dorothy and I. We related so well as girls during the training. I wouldn't eat food without sharing with any of them. What made it better was the fact that we were from the same areas, that's Beitbridge and Gwanda. These two towns share a lot in terms of culture and other such dynamics. We used to share stories in SeSotho, isiNdebele, and tshiVenda languages. We shared that sisterhood spirit. This was our daily life at Nampundwe camp.

Completing the registration process became our first involvement at Nampundwe Camp. As for daily routines, we woke up early, did toyi-toyi and later attended lessons. Lessons differed from day to day depending on the instructor of the day. What never changed were the early morning exercises and physical military drills. We were taught respect, truthfulness, honesty, and bravery in facing the enemy. We were taught to have mercy, a tactic of fighting without compromising or making the guerrilla vulnerable. We were so sensitive. Our stay in Nampundwe Camp was short-lived. We were later taken to Zambia, Mwembeshi camp. In our first [time] in Mwembeshi, lessons were divided into packaged sessions. There was physical which consisted of toyi-toyi, and other military

---

[7] Grace Muchachi was among the first group of nine female combatants to receive ZPRA's military training. Refer to her full interview which is also included in this publication.

drills. The second was the political commissariat that focused on the ideology of the party and the army. Emphasis was that the party and the army were two distinct units in operations but logically the party was higher than the army as it is the party that produces the army and not vice-versa.

We were taught that our main objective was to fight the colonial system and any obstacles that it championed. The aim was not to kill wantonly. The lessons made it clear that we did not wage a war with the whites because they are whites but because of their system of discrimination, brutality, white monopoly and white privilege. Such a lesson was re-emphasized every day so that we do not see whites as enemies, but their system as an obstacle for realizing the full potential of the black community.

We trained with men, there was not a single case or a scenario when we were separated from men in the training. We did almost everything that was done by our male counterparts. For example, we did obstacles, judo, shooting range, and all ammunition gun lessons. I did all types of guns in our lessons. We were taught how to assemble, shoot range and how we should operate and what to do when the gun has jammed. That is why after coming from Morogoro I was able to teach other men and females at Mwembeshi as an instructor. That's how when I was posted back to Mwembeshi, after Morogoro, I was able to teach men and women the same teaching that I received. Ironically, I instructed men who ended up fighting in the war front although I did not go. Can you say we did not play a role? When we taught those that went to the front.

I don't see why some people would say women never played a part or a role when in fact I gave knowledge and skills to the same men who fought in the war front. At the end of the day, people think that fighting involved just carrying a gun in the war front. That's not true, fighting was a process that involved stages from recruitment, training, deployment, and actual fighting. Everyone had their role and share while those in the party led in policy and administrative work which involved the army and struggle. In all those stages women played a role in the administration, instructors, intelligence. This is why others were able to come out from Mkushi camp after bombardment by the enemy. This was a result of the training.

People think that we went to war to be singers, cooks, and entertain guerrillas. If singing was done, it was done as war cries in toyi-toyi exercises and not as a separate activity. The only difference is that we as female guerrillas did not go to the front but if the war persisted, we could have been posted. That's my thinking. But I remember, when we were in Mwembeshi Joshua Nkomo requested that we should be pulled off military training so that we go to school. His thinking had been that the training was too hard for us as girls but we refused. Because we had protocols our refusal was not a confrontation with him, we were telling our instructors that we wanted to continue. ZPRA taught us to respect protocols. Besides, imagine a fifteen-year-old telling ZAPU President that they do not want to take orders.

In Morogoro, we stayed in a dormitory setup while men stayed in the tents. Before more people came to Morogoro we had our own rooms stocked with food although we had our main kitchen which we shared with ZANLA guerrillas. Instructors stayed near us to guard against miscellaneous activities that would happen like raids and forced sexual activities. Such did not happen, maybe it happened behind closed doors. In my view, instructors did not use ranks to gain sexual favours. But I cannot rule out that it may have happened. Truly speaking in our group this did not happen. Maybe in other groups. Although ZPRA's policy safeguarded recruits, stories of sexual intercourse and rape were rumoured. As you know, some of these were adults. There was a heavy penalty on those that broke laws, policies, and procedures.

In Morogoro we took six months to train in accordance with ZPRA's training policy. You would wonder why we got retrained in Morogoro. It is because we failed to have six months of training at Mwembeshi because of ZIPA consideration and failed to have six months under ZIPA in Mgagao because of infighting that led to a crisis when we were attacked by ZANLA.

We trained at Mwembeshi for almost three months, but it was later discovered that Zimbabwean military forces cannot train differently when in fact they are fighting for one cause. It was then that they formed ZIPA which was supposed to be a joint military training at Mgagao. This joint training failed to take off as members of ZANLA attacked ZPRA and we retaliated. I think forty-something of our ZPRA forces died.

We were attacked and ran away because we did not have guns and worse off we were newcomers in their training camp at Mgagao. We managed to flee like we were trained to. Those three months at Mwembeshi helped us a lot. They were fighting using guns and grenades. We ran for hours until midnight. We stopped when we arrived at a police station called Iringa prison. The party decided to retract us from Mgagao as joint training had failed. We then went to Morogoro to receive training there as ZPRA forces. I think we were attacked because they were intimidated by our level of organisation. Besides, ZANU was formed on a tribal approach of the Shona-hegemony while ZAPU was nationalist in character, inclusive of every tribe in Zimbabwe. That's why it was called ZAPU, 'P' representing people as it was a union of every tribe.

ZANU under Robert Mugabe never liked us. I get angry and frustrated when I hear of this thing called ZANU. I went to war thinking that our lives would be improved, but alas we are all suffering, those that went to war and those who did not. The state had a subjective way of vetting those that were supposed to get benefits. ZPRA was a government in waiting, we had engineers and pilots. We were not surprised when they attacked us in Mgagao as they felt intimidated by the kind of training and military management system we had.

The crisis or attack in Mgagao started a week after Joshua Nkomo's visit with members of his command structure. During his visit, it was brought to Joshua

Nkomo's attention that ZPRA guerrillas were not given adequate food whenever ZANU was on cooking duty. The food rationing had not gone down well with us because we had also contributed towards food that was supposed to be provided to everyone during the training. Joshua asserted that he was going to address the problem with his colleagues, high command cadres from ZANLA that included the late Retired General Solomon 'Rex Nhongo' Mujuru.

A few days after the high command from both parties had left, we thought everything had been resolved. Unbeknown to us that the worst was to come. While at the kitchen waiting for food to be served, there was a delay and we had to wait. As soldiers, we couldn't oppose or argue but we had to take the command as it was. Also, our instructors requested us to be patient. While waiting for food, instructors ordered us to perform military drills and gun assembly tactics. The female company which was company 'A' started the activity. It was a test to see our swiftness in assembling the guns. We stripped the guns, assembled, and held them the way the instructor wanted us to. We did this while the ZANLA counterparts were watching. They felt threatened and amazed. One of them passed a comment saying *"Vanhu ava vaka-trainer mhani, vachatipedza"* (These people are well trained, and if we are not careful, they will advance to us and kill us in no time).

What made them scared was the fact that they never expected such from female recruits and worse we were the only females from ZPRA and ZANLA. So other companies followed the same exercise of gun assembly activities. Again the onlookers where shocked and amazed.

While the ZANLA guerrillas were watching us, we held an obstacle training that involved jumping over high obstacles. They began to pass remarks that, *'Vanhu ava vaka-trainer mhani, vachatipedza tese apa, zvirinani kuti tivapedzese isusu* (these people are well trained, there is a likelihood that they will finish us all. We need to deal with them before they advance to us). Our instructors ordered us to stop after they overheard such remarks and also picked up using their skill of intelligence that their counterparts were not happy and felt intimidated.

Our instructors ordered us to dismiss, go and bath then return later for supper. When we arrived at the kitchen later that day, we found that there was no food left for us after ZANLA had fed its guerrillas. Our company was the first on ZPRA's side to receive food. When we heard this we went outside to tell other companies that there wasn't any food left for us. Male guerrillas went and found no food. A small group of females decided to go to the tents to get food from logistics officers. This was mainly tinned foods. Some guerrillas were waiting to inquire why food had run out. While I was still at the tents with girls, we heard the commotion, noise of people shouting. The noise appeared like people who were jostling for something.

Suddenly, I heard two gunshots. The crisis had reached another level. We saw our male guerrillas running away from the kitchen while guns were fired. As female recruits, we joined our team in heading out of the camp. Two of our instructors were attacked and died on the spot. One called Lemmy got chopped by an axe. The other called Ndumba was shot. These two were relaxed, not thinking that such was going to happen. It's not like they were weak, no, they were caught unaware.

One of the instructors called Stanley Elish Gagisa Nleya[8] took over to command the crisis after sensing that we were going to perish, especially considering that we were not armed. He then commanded the scene while we were running away. He commanded like we were now at the front. He would say, crawl, take ground, crawl, up, run. He was seeing what the ZANLA were doing. He was able to tell us to look at the back and receive the grenades so as to throw them back. We did as commanded. We would catch the grenades and throw them back within thirty seconds. The safety pins would have already been removed from the grenades. They felt the heat. They had thought it could have been a stroll in the park. They were lucky that we did not have guns.

They wasted their ammunition as we managed to evade the obstacle. We continued running until we arrived at Iringa police station. We stayed there for a while as the party was formalizing that we move to Morogoro. After the training at Morogoro, Grace Muchachi and I were sent back to Mwembeshi as instructors to train the second group of girls. We were officially instructors. We trained both male and female recruits. I still recall the second group had fifty-three girls, if am not mistaken. We also did not separate recruits.

I think we were taken back to Mwembeshi as instructors to be an inspiration to the new female recruits. It was a way to motivate them to soldier on. The party used us as an inspiration to young girls on how high up the ranks they could rise. As a company instructor, I used to take my company for a toyi-toyi, exercise and military drill. I would dismiss them around 7am.

I was later assigned to Kafue Camp in Zambia and took the role of a camp commander for a typing camp. I was deputized by a lady who was a contemporary like the likes of Jane Lungile Ngwenya. Her name was Ms. Nyamurohwa. She was later made the camp commander and I deputized her. What is important to note is that, although Nyamurohwa never received military training, she was elevated based on seniority. ZAPU or ZPRA prioritized seniority and loyalty.

By the end of 1978 I was transferred to Victory Camp, which was a transit camp where I was now responsible for selecting, registering, and training female recruits. This was important as we would identify those that were not genuine. Part of my role was also to pick up intelligence information of what was

---

[8] Stanley Elish Gagisa Nleya was a senior ZPRA's military instructor who trained both men and female combatants upon. He further went for various operations at the height of the liberation struggle. Refer to his full interview which is also included in this publication.

happening at home using information form recruits.

I remember before the bombing at Mkushi, Joshua had come to Victory Camp and ordered me to go to Mkushi to train others similarly as I had been trained, there was particular emphasis on physical training. Unfortunately, Mkushi was bombed and I could not go and conduct the trainings. Part of the initial group of nine girls had proceeded to Cuba for further training. Audrey and Jane were deployed to Mkushi.

After the war, we landed at Bulawayo Airport, now Joshua Mqabuko Nkomo International Airport, and we were taken to Luveve camp. I was demobilized and never integrated into the then newly formed Zimbabwe National Army. We were then discharged back to our homes. When I arrived home, my family ran away from me including my mother. I tried to remind them who I was but it still took a while before they recognised me.

I stayed at home for some time and decided to join other women at the ZPRA camp at Sierra assembly point situated in the Insukamini area near the city of Gweru in the Midlands Province of Zimbabwe. The camp hosted all former ZPRA women guerrilla camps that got attested into the army and others that were demobilized from the army. I went there because ZAPU had asked those that had not been integrated to work for the party. Despite that things did not go the way I expected them to be in post-independent Zimbabwe, I do not regret joining the liberation struggle.

CHAPTER 3

'At the end, they recognized our efforts and we became a brigade, I became the commander'

Getrude Mpala

(Cuban trained cadre and commander of the women's brigade)

Fig 7: Freedom Fighter, Getrude Mpala, who was trained in Cuba. After the training, she was appointed commander of ZPRA's women brigade. In 1980 she was integrated into the then newly formed Zimbabwe National Army.

My name is Sibonokuhle Ngwenya. I was born in 1960. In the mid-1970s there were various agitations about the brutality of the colonial regime and the need to decolonize. Stories from our elders often inspired us to denounce colonial repression. As youths, we would meet, attend rallies and listen to stories of liberation on the radio. Some radio programs were presented by Jane Ngwenya.

We used to listen as she invited people to join the liberation struggle. The biggest recruitment was at the funeral of Jason Ziyaphapha Moyo, after which there was a mass exodus of recruits joining the struggle. His death led many young people to be fired up to join the struggle. I was 17years old at the time and I joined the liberation struggle.

My journey to the war began when six men and I boarded a bus from Bulawayo to take us to Botswana. The bus took off using Gwanda road but it reached a point along the way where it couldn't proceed because of heavy rains. The swampy clay soils made navigation very difficult too. We were told to get off the bus. We hid under trees but it was in vain. A short while later we proceeded to move towards Shashi River with the intention of crossing over to Botswana from there. We hoped that after crossing over to Botswana we would start asking for directions to refugee camps.

Unfortunately, when we reached Shashi, the river was full and very rough. We couldn't cross. I did not know how to swim. We tried to walk along the bank to find a shallower entry point but it was to no avail. While in search of a shallower entry point, we found a homestead just at the edge of the river. That homestead had a family and I think they would occasionally help people to cross the river. They told us that we needed to wait two or three days for the river to subside. As the only girl, I was told to go inside the hut and help other girls cook.

We managed to stay there two nights and finally crossed over to Botswana on the third day. While walking, we asked people where those intending to join the struggle headed. They told us to head in the direction of Bobonong. When we reached Bobonong villagers told us that we were late and the lorry that ferried people had left. Fortunately, a tractor came by. The tractor was going to Selibe-Phikwe. We sat in the trailer and were taken to the police camp. From the camp we were escorted to the prison and stayed there. We spent two nights at the prison. There was communication with colleagues in ZPRA. We then moved to Francistown and it is then that I began to see one or two people that I knew. The next day recruits flew to Victor Camp in Lusaka. When we arrived at VC, the camp had not grown in numbers as there were young kids, teenagers, women, and the elderly. VC was a semi-training camp. Exercises, parades, and military drills were conducted while the command element planned what to do with recruits. Only those that were physically fit would be seconded for military training. The elderly would remain behind to take care of young kids.

I was then chosen to go to Havana, Cuba to train as a female combatant. I went with those that were going to pursue their academic studies, advanced military intelligence, and other key positions within the army. We moved to Angola and travelled to Cuba by ship. It was a long journey. Upon completing the training, which lasted about six to eight months, I came back to Lusaka and worked [at the] strategic ZPRA Headquarters, which was known as Entabeni. I was more of an interpreter working closely with Cubans and Russians. I was assigned to be a focal person in the working projects with Cubans and Russians. Part of my job was to interpret Cuban documents and also coordinate their programs as you might know that they facilitated a lot of aid in terms of humanitarian and human development especially in medical training and other military works. At that office, I worked with a woman combatant called Madeline Tshawe- the wife of McCloud Tshawe, a former ZPRA Intelligence Officer.

During the renowned bombardments, I was working in Lusaka, Zambia. It was a terrible experience as most of the strategic offices and zones were targeted and ultimately bombed. The army strategized once more and female combatants were then taken to Kafue while other male combatants that were still at training were all deployed to the front. The army saw it possible to deploy all of them to the front as it was better for them to carry out operations than to die in the camps. There was a lot of movement in trying to find new modalities.

With time, a new camp was opened in Solwezi to accommodate both men and women. Women and men had their exclusive camps. All trained female combatants were taken to Solwezi camp. Solwezi was a swampy camp where it rained throughout. Female combatants survived the harsh environment now that they were accomplished soldiers. While men were deployed to the front, female combatants were deployed to guard the rear. During the time of going to Solwezi, the party and army decided to form a women's brigade that was not for operations but to organize assignments and deployment in the rear. Since it was now the final push, the safety of ZPRA in the liberated zones depended on women hence it was seen to categorize women and form a brigade to discharge such duties.

I was appointed as the brigade commander. Others that I got appointed with were; deputy commander Olie Ngwenya (Ossie Sibanda), currently she is the Bulawayo District Commander and she is now a colonel; Chief of Staff Chiratidzo Iris Mabuwa served in various portfolios as a minister; Commissar Martha Dube; Chief of Staff Thabisile Moyo and Training Personnel Ntombiyezizweni Sibanda. Monica Mnguni, Moratiwa Gazi (Abigail Mabetha), Jester Nleya, Nompumelelo Moyo (Gift Tichatonga), Mavis Nyathi, and Sebenzile Sigoge were responsible for catering, transport, artillery, engineering, communication and Security/reconnaissance, respectively.

Fig 8: Picture of Marshal Mpofu with Getrude Mpala (women brigade commander) at Sierra Assembly Point in Gweru. **Picture source**: Accessed from Getrude's personal archive.

20

CHAPTER 4

'I thought of others first before myself. This is what the liberation struggle taught us to be!'

Hazel Ndlovu
(Mwembeshi trained cadre)

Fig 9: Freedom Fighter, Hazel Ndlovu, who was trained at Mwembeshi. She received further training in Cuba in military intelligence. She later joined the police force and served diligently. She is retired.

My name is Hazel Sibanda, although Lynna Nyoni is the name that I was given at birth. My war name was Hazel Ndlovu but I still maintained the name till today. I was born in 1959 in Botswana. I joined the war while I was seventeen years old in 1976. I spent my entire childhood in Botswana. I was brought up by my maternal grandfather who migrated from Zimbabwe to Botswana. My mother was a housemaid in the then Rhodesia working in low density suburbs and my father was a Kalanga based in Botswana with full citizenship. They were never together with my mother.

I did my primary school at Sikakano School at Francistown, Botswana and proceeded to do secondary school at Tutume McConnel Community College where I did form one to three. During that time in Botswana, form three was considered the Ordinary Level and others would proceed to do form four to five which was considered Advanced level.

After completing form three, I went back home as I waited for my results. I had also applied to a nursing school in Gaborone. Initially, I had told my parents that I wanted to pursue nursing as a career. However, I ended up joining the liberation struggle of Zimbabwe at the Zimbabwe House in Botswana where there was a guy called *Mnyamana or Black Swine*[9]. I was inspired to join the liberation [struggle] by my mother's cousin called Ndebele. He was an already trained ZPRA combatant who used to come to visit my grandfather together with some of his friends on their way to the operational areas. I used to admire their combat gear and felt inspired so much that while I had the aspiration of becoming a nurse, I was now wishing to become a soldier. Mnyamana knew me, he knew my family background, my family and grandfather.

In one of my visits to the Zimbabwe House to see Mnyamana, I told him that I wanted to join the liberation struggle, he simply told his colleagues this one (referring to me) should not go to the transit camp, the moment she goes there her grandfather is likely to come and drag her out of the camp. They told me to wait for a day or two. This was done so that I was flown to Zambia without undergoing the transit camp process. The day came and I joined others that were coming from Zimbabwe and flew to Zimbabwe. I'm told my grandfather wanted to follow me shortly after the plane had taken off. It is alleged that when they told him that I had flown, showing him the plane that I had left with, he fell and fainted for a while. I think this was because he did not want me to join the liberation struggle.

We arrived at Nampundwe; I don't quite remember the month. On arrival, I realized that a lot had changed. Stories of those that were coming from Zimbabwe, then Rhodesia, made me realize that this required a lot of commitment. I remember some would burst into tears when narrating how they were recruited and their journey to Zambia. I had taken the process lightly because I voluntarily joined with no one forcing me. Upon arrival in Zambia, I was named Hazel. Names were changed to hide identity and protect the identity of people that one had left behind. As recruits we would eat together. We never undermined each other. We ate tinned food and other types of foods that were new to me like beans and fish that tasted very bitter. With time I got used to it.

We moved to Mwembeshi together with our male counterparts. If my memory serves me right, our male counterparts were around 2 000 and we were at least 100 and we were the last group to be trained at Mwembeshi. People in Mwembeshi were disciplined. Men had their tents opposite women. This was

---

[9]His real name was Elliot Sibanda and was the intelligence officer based in Botswana at the time when he was captured by the Rhodesian Selous Scouts.

done to minimize improper association of men and women in the camp.

We would wake up early in the morning for a run, military drills, and other physical training. It was very difficult for one to do these if you were not used to it. Many would faint, including men. In some of the trainings one was supposed to carry a stick resembling a gun. You would be told to carry that stick [where] ever one would go. This was mainly done for us to get used to carrying a gun. We were later issued with guns. At times, after the run we would do frog jumps depending on the day's instructor. Among the male instructors, there was Stanley Gagisa, Eddie Sigoge, and among the female instructors there was Audrey, Bvundzai, and Grace. We never trained in separate groups. Men and women were trained as one. We did almost everything that was done by men. Female instructors became our role models and gave us the much-needed inspiration. Bvundzai was so tough, she would do a forward fall that would leave us in awe.

After the military drills, we would go for breakfast. Meal times were timed. When the whistle was blown, you would have to immediately join others for the next assignment, even if you had not yet been served or eaten your food. It was the same with bath times. You needed to be punctual and manage time wisely. We would also do commissariat lessons that emphasized the history of the nation and the objective of the liberation struggle. We were made to hate the colonial system but not the whites as people. We were taught to hate the system and coexist with those that are accommodative to the black majority. It made us see the real objective of joining the struggle.

Among the female recruits that trained with me at Mwembeshi; there was Zeigue, Ingrid, Samkeliso, Sylvia, Dorcas, and Cecelia. I seem to be forgetting others. I remember Samkeliso who was once captured by the whites in Botswana together with Black Swine. They were later released shortly before independence.

After completing the training at Mwembeshi, more selections were made and from our group, a number were chosen to do further training in military intelligence and close security. From our group, twenty were chosen and I was part of those selected to enroll for a six-month military intelligence. We traveled from Lusaka to Luanda in Angola. Some were held up in Angola while they received treatment for various ailments. Those that remained in Angola flew to Cuba but the group I was in traveled by sea for a duration of twenty-one days. The group that traveled by air reached Cuba ahead of us.

We returned to Zambia soon after completing our six-month course. For some time, I was deployed at Zimbabwe House where I worked with the intelligence department. As time progressed, I think after a month the department of intelligence opened an office under the University of Zambia in Lusaka that was called the Vatican. However, Sibonginkosi Gumede, affectionately known as JB, and I stayed at a flat in Kwabata. JB was the young sister of Ndumiso Gumede, a football technocrat. We worked under the direct supervision of Dumiso

Dabengwa. We were ordered to stay in Kwabata as other cabins had highly classified information. It was an arrangement to decongest sensitive information from the Zimbabwe House. The arrangement was that everyday Solly, the driver, would come to the flat to collect us early in the morning and ferry us to the Vatican offices.

On one day Solly delayed coming to pick us up from our residence. We wondered wjat could have delayed him but we had no one to ask. Looking over the balcony, while waiting for Solly, I saw big helicopters coming from the northwestern side. I quickly called out, '*JB, JB come see enemy army!*' In Cuba we had been taught how to identify a helicopter that was armed for a mission regardless of the direction it was facing. There's a certain way in which it flies when on a mission. I could sense trouble that day. JB came running and confirmed that which I was seeing. When Solly finally arrived, he explained to us that he had been sent on some errands by Dumiso Dabengwa. When we arrived at the camp, we found dead bodies of some officers that we worked with. It became clear to us that if we had been picked up on time by Solly we would have been part of those that were attacked and killed. No one at the office survived the attack.

The helicopters had simultaneously bombed Vatican, Freedom Camp, and Mkushi. The bombardment had started. At that time there were no cellphones for us to quickly convey a message about the attack. It was a well-orchestrated plan and I believe there were people among us who were feeding them with information. I'm told in Mkushi the targets were Jane Ndlovu and Audrey. They had been singled out and called by name. How did the enemy know their names? How do you explain a scenario of betrayal and information leaking? Anyway, this was the war, it happens. I also remember another attack when we had attended an Afro-Asian Peoples' Solidarity Organization (AAPSO) conference in Nakatinde Hall. Joshua Nkomo was present and so was Lookout Masuku and his wife. Lookout was attacked but he survived. I was once seconded to join Samkeliso but later another instruction was issued saying I stay in Lusaka. At Mkushi I had been chosen to be an instructor but later withdrawn in order to further my training. It was all about luck and God.

As we approached 1979 a lot of people were sent back home. A few came by plane, I think these are the ones that came with Joshua, and others by train and road. I came by road and I was deployed at Vanguard House in Harare where I worked. I was in charge of seconding and later recruiting female combatants for police training. They all came through me. I had to second a lot of them to the police training. There was a guy who was a sergeant major at the depot and I was in constant communication with him after I had recommended the female combatants for police training. One day he said to me, '*Ko iwe musikana how old are you*?' (Young lady how old are you). I responded to him by telling him my age and he had to reply to me here and there and said, 'Why do you send people for police training when you are seated there with the requisite qualifications of being a police officer? That's how I joined the police and later went for police training. I thought of others more than myself. This is what war taught us! Shortly, before the training, I went for demobilization at Sierra Assembly point near Gweru and later returned to Harare for training.

When I completed the training, I was deployed to West Commonage at Mpophoma as they encouraged all former freedom fighters to work close to their relatives as they had spent more time in the bush. At that point, I was now a police officer. I stayed with my maternal relatives at Mpophoma. Remember, I told you that my war name was Hazel Ndlovu, I had to continue using Hazel as it had become so popular but I became Sibanda as I had to use the surname of my uncle who was the cousin to my mother. He was called Phineas *Stina* Sibanda. That's how I turned out to be a Sibanda. I was later transferred to Njube Station, Mzilikazi Station, Victoria Falls Station, Lupane Station, Victoria Falls, and later posted in Hwange for 12 years. I came back and worked Bulawayo Central, Hillside Station and by then I was now promoted. My last station was at Magwegwe Police station where I was now the officer in charge and ultimately retired from there. I am a mother of four boys.

Fig 10: (Left side picture): Grace Muchachi (left) with Hazel Ndlovu (right) at the back yard of Zimbabwe House in Lusaka. **Picture source**: Accessed from Grace's personal archive.

PICTURES OF VICTORY CAMP

Pictures below show the lifestyle of women in Victory Camp where they stayed prior to selection for military training. Pictures used in this publication were accessed from Zenzo Nkobi Collection kept at Mafela Trust and South African History Archive (SAHA).

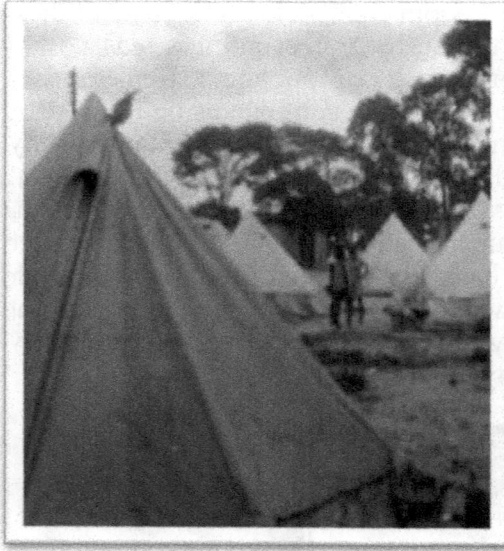

Fig 11: Tents that accommodated refugees at VC.

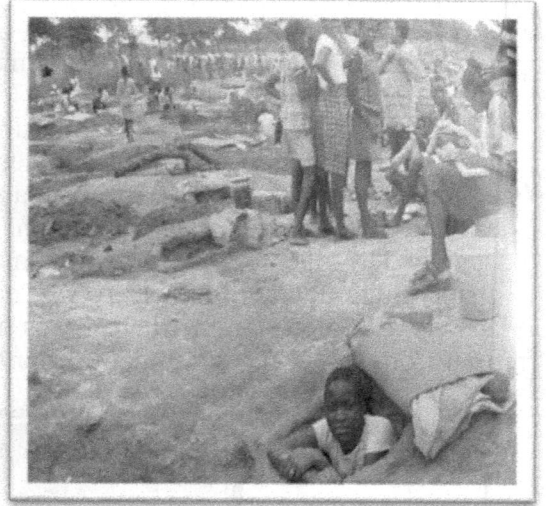

Fig 12: Girls relaxing with one looking out from a defense pit.

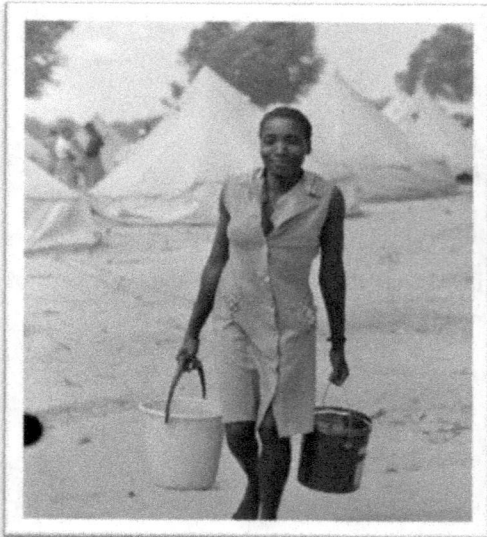

Fig 13: A girl carrying buckets of water in Victory Camp.

Fig 14: Clean water is delivered to Victory Camp by truck

CHAPTER 5

'Training with men made me realize that women can do everything that men did!'

Zegeu Mpofu
(Mwembeshi trained cadre)

Fig 15: Freedom Fighter, Zegeu Mpofu, who was trained at Mwembeshi. She became security personnel at Victory Camp and was later sent for advanced military intelligence, counter-intelligence, and espionage training in Cuba. Upon coming back from Cuba, she was one of the pioneer instructors in opening a military intelligence school in Kitwe. She was deployed to accompany casualties from Mkushi and other bombardments to Poland as an intelligence officer. In 1980 she was integrated into the then newly formed Zimbabwe National Army.

My name is Sesinyana Grace Mlotshwa. My war name became Zegeu Mpofu. Zegeu-four (ZGU) is a gun with four barrels and it can go up to six barrels. I was born in a family of four children; two girls and two boys. I did my primary level at Matole and Silima Primary Schools. I pursued my secondary education at Luveve Secondary School in Bulawayo.

I joined the liberation struggle in 1976 when I had visited my rural home Emzinmyama village in Plumtree. I went to fetch water at a nearby well in the company of my paternal aunt Senzeni Mhlanga. The well was a few meters from home. While at the well we saw my mother running towards us. This was a time when parents were very strict and they could easily beat us so we go frightened as she came closer. Panting she told us that there were two gun wielding men outside our home who were looking for young people to join the liberation struggle. She was worried and told us to leave aside the water that we had fetched to run to the nearby pit to hide. We ran and hid there for some time.

We stayed for a while in the pit and we could faintly hear some of the conversations between the soldiers and community members. The soldiers mentioned recruitment young people to fight the colonial system. I was hit by the temptation to approach them and volunteer to train as a soldier. I stood up to peep at them. Indeed, they fitted my mother's description. They were wearing khaki-like trousers, putting on very long coats and carried guns. At that point, I felt like jumping out from the pit to tell them of my desire to join the war. I was prepared to do exactly that. When you are young you get ambitious at times! I then told Senzeni of my intentions. She tried to deter me but I maintained my stance. I added that I was not going to tell them that she was hiding there.

I came out of the pit enthused and proceeded straight to the soldiers. I found them talking to my male cousin and a maternal aunt of mine. I did not interrupt their conversation. I greeted them and remained standing there listening to their conversation. They explained why they had come to our village and who they had recruited to fight the colonial system. I found myself having blurted out that I wanted to join the liberation struggle. The first question they asked me was where I live. After I responded they laughed telling me that they had been to my home and they saw an old lady. They described my mother. They promised to pick me up from home once they were done with errands. Senzeni finally came out of the pit and found us wrapping up the conversation. We carried our abandoned buckets of water and went back home.

We waited from around 11am to around 4pm for the soldiers to return. Many young boys and girls came to join us. The soldiers had directed them to wait at our home for easy coordination. The gathering grew to about a hundred young people. Soldiers returned around 4pm and instructed us to follow their route. They identified themselves as Bhobho and Lizwe. I don't know if these were real names or liberation names.

The long-awaited journey started. We moved as a group; on some paths we ran. We passed Osabeni, and Sivaka. Between 6 and 7pm we had reached the border separating Zimbabwe and Botswana. We were instructed to crawl underneath the barbed wire. The two men who had suddenly become very harsh ordered that we help each other to cross. The instruction that followed was that we should run and not look back at all. We ran until we were intercepted by another team of recruiters. We reached some part of the bush where we slept for a while. This was around 12 midnight.

Around 4am recruiters instructed us to wake up and run towards the main road. Two of them led until we met lorries with Botswana number plates. We quickly had to jumped into the lorries which took us to the prison. When we got there, we registered our names and requested to give brief introductions of ourselves, families and opine on the situation at home vis-à-vis colonial repression. I think such was going to inform their reconnaissance. We only spent a night there and the next morning we were taken to Francistown which was a transit camp. We slept there I think for three or so days. A lot had changed in terms of our lifestyle.

On the fourth day at Francistown, names were called out and mine was included. We were told to board four big lorries that had parked outside. There was a parade before boarding and that is when we were informed that we were departing for Zambia. We left by plane to Zambia and arrived at the Lusaka airport. Big lorries were already outside waiting for us. There was a lot going on, I felt confused as to where we were going and coming from. I was disoriented. The lorries ferried us to Nampundwe. We arrived in Nampundwe at night.

At 4am a whistle was blown; we woke up and went to parade where we were informed that we needed to prepare to welcome Joshua Nkomo at the airport. We all got excited that we were about to physically meet someone we had heard so much about at home. A wooden drum container was opened during the parade and it had uniforms inside. The uniforms were damp and lice infested. We wore the uniforms regardless of how ill-fitting some of them were. This is when it dawned on me that my life had changed. Three instructors led us as we ran in our uniforms. Instructors had announced that we were going to welcome Nkomo at the airport unbeknown to us that it was a planned long-distance run. We run so fast almost 15kms. Along the way, some were fainting, vomiting, and others lagging behind. You would reach a point then return as fast as you could. Personally, it was very hard for me because I was not used to physical exercise at all. We assembled at the parade point while waiting for others to join us. As soon as others had returned, we proceeded to a nearby mountain where we were taught to climb a mountain using frog jumps. This was a struggle.

Instructors had become harsher and did not negotiate with anyone. We jumped and at the tip of the mountain, we were told to roll down with our hands between our feet. We did all that and as soon as we reached the foot of the mountain, we were instructed to go to a parade point and sit down. An instruction for us to go for breakfast followed but no one stood up. Everyone was exhausted. Real-life had started. Instructors laughed at how everyone failed to get up. They then began commissariat lessons. There was a clear connection between the mountain exercise and the lesson when they started highlighting the objectives of joining the liberation struggle.

That very night, big lorries came and we were told to board those lorries. We still had that confusion and exhaustion from the physical exercise. Instructors called us by name into the trucks and we traveled from Nampundwe to Mwembeshi. That night we pitched our tents and were put into companies. The site of the camp was close to a river, this made the place cold.

The next morning training began and there was no fun. Companies ranged from A up to H. I think in a platoon you would get one woman because we were around one hundred and fifty out of over five hundred men. What made the training difficult was the fact that we were not separated from men. Training with men made me realize that what men can do could be done by women too. We performed all tactics that they did. The training included learning commissariat lessons of the objectives of the war, gun stripping and assembly, how to use guns, topography, range, judo, crossing of rivers, crossing of obstacles and a lot of long distance running. I remember one of the instructors, Eddie Sigoge, used to fire live bullets during the obstacle crossing. It was scary.

Early mornings were only meant to promote physical fitness through running, exercise and judo. After those, we would come back and break for breakfast and later return to the parade. After the parade, we would then dismiss into companies for other lessons that required a classroom setup in order to commissariat, strip guns and assembly, learn how to use guns, and topography among other things. This depended on the program of the day.

Some of the women that I trained with included Hazel, Susan, Viola, Samkeliso, Vivian, Moddie, Beauty 'Bhuzhwa', Silver, Anna, Ingrid, Soffie, Dorcas, Thandiwe, and Sakhile. There were other trained women combatants that had completed their training at Morogoro and had been deployed as instructors. There was Grace, Bvundzai, Constance, Belinda, Peasant, and Audrey. These women instructors were men in women figures. All I'm trying to say is they were bold. Their level of effort was similar to that of male instructors.

I remember one time during a parade Stanley Gagisa Nleya and Philip Valerio Sibanda publicly acknowledged that there was no difference between what was taught by women instructors and what they taught. These female instructors instructed everyone, including men! We looked up to them and aspired to be like them as soon as we completed our training. They were so encouraging and we envied them that indeed what a woman can do a man can do. There was no distinction to what we were taught by men. Stanley Gagisa specialized in physical training and would be so tough on us. On some days he would standing and watch while Valerio Sibanda or Constance took over. This was war. There was also the command element. The camp commander was Eddie Sigoge. Other instructors included Ananias Gwenzi (Philip Valerio Sibanda), Moses Phinda, Stanley Doko Gagisa, Arab, Magadlela, Doctor Mbeya, Sibangani, Jockey, Ethan, Ntatshana and Maphara,

At Mwembeshi we ate beans, buns that we called *amanyunyumane* and sour milk that would have initially been powdered. There was *isitshwala*, tinned fish and on some days, there was game meat. When we completed the guerrilla training, we also did a bit of regular training and completed the training by 1977. I have forgotten the specific month. Quite a number of us trained women combatants were deployed to Victory Camp to be security personnel. The camp was now an exclusive transit camp for only women, teenagers, and young kids that we called *okijana*. VC was a camp that was left behind by the Angolans and its original name was in Portuguese and loosely translated to 'Victory is certain'. This explains why it was later called Victory Camp. I was one of those that provided security services as guards and did all security protocols that included vetting those coming in to stay inside the camp. At that time, I was in possession of an AK-47 although there were also men that were in our security department who were doing anti-air security outside the camp.

At Victory Camp, the camp commander was Cecil Ndanga, the commissar was Saul popularly known as 'Professor'. While at VC I was among those that were chosen for further training in Cuba for military intelligence, counter intelligence and espionage. The aim was to improve understanding how information is gathered in various contexts and how one can perform a task to counter anything in that context. Espionage involved the art of information gathering in a spy-type of scenario, leaking it, and releasing it to achieve a certain intended outcome. It was only women that convened in Cuba although we were coming from different departments. There was Lydia, Ndlela, Silver, Hazel, Sibophile, Cecil, Mario, Phineas and I among others. We traveled to Angola and we took a plane to Cuba while Hazel and crew traveled by ship. The good thing is we all arrived safely and learned together.

We completed our training in 1978 and came back to Zambia. I was tasked to open an intelligence training school in Kitwe according to recommendations I received based on my performance in my studies. Only Ndlela, Mike and I had done military intelligence in Bulgaria. That military intelligence school was opened and I became a senior instructor. We trained the first group of other cadres that had completed their six months of training and in the second group, we then targeted all those cadres from other departments especially men that were going to the front. As we were still in the training the bombardments started. Many people died and others sustained serious injuries. There were plans for those that had sustained injuries to receive medical treatment overseas. All those who were going for treatment to Poland were accompanied by me to afford me the opportunity to monitor and gather intelligence information. I was on a mission to monitor and gather information as an intelligence officer. This was now my role. I was disguised as someone going there to receive medical. We stayed there for about four months, some were treated and given artificial legs, succored and bandaged.

Time went by, I was seconded once more together with four other women that were coming from Namibia to do a nursing course in Poland. These women were Peninnah, Elina, Florence, Elma. We did state-certified nursing. During that time when we were doing our nursing course, ZAPU had a representative in Poland who was called Hitler Chenjerai Hunzvi. We used to go to his offices to receive orientations and be updated on the liberation situation back home. Hunzvi loved talking and orienting everyone about what was taking place at home. People would gather at his offices during weekends. There are some that we would meet in his offices who had come to do other assignments and courses in Poland.

These included Chipo Daughters Mabuwa, Ester, Sipho, Eugen, and Peter.

There were however some challenges in Poland at that time as cases of racism were so high. Some whites in Poland would pass racist comments about black people. Others genuinely marveled when they met a black person physically. During this time *'Richman poor man'* by Kunta Kinte was very popular. Everywhere you moved you would be called, 'Kunta Kinte.' They never liked us. You could not bath in public rest rooms in Poland without white people running and flocking to see your nakedness and try to find the baboon characteristics in you. It was frustrating. Others would interrogate me and dispute that I am African because I was light in complexion. They named me *wander musica*. This meant a very beautiful girl but directly translated it was a female calf of a mule. Still such, remained demeaning to me and others like me.

I left Poland for Zimbabwe via Zambia in 1980. Some of my peers had already been in Zimbabwe. I went to Greendale Harare and worked as a shopkeeper in one of the stores that belonged to Joshua Nkomo. I was integrated into the then newly formed Zimbabwe National Army. I led a normal life, got married and had three children.

CHAPTER 6

'I thought I had made it in life after seeing lights at the airport but the worst was to come'

Cecelia Sibanda
(Mwembeshi trained cadre)

Fig 16: Freedom Fighter, Cecelia Sibanda, was trained at Mwembeshi. She served as security personnel operating under National Security Organization (NSO) and later survived bombardment at Mkushi when she had gone for a fact-finding mission. She later joined the police force and served diligently until her retirement.

My real name is Grace Maphosa, my war name was Cecelia Sibanda. I was born in the year 1962, in Plumtree in a village called Tjehanga. I spent my childhood in Plumtree. I completed both primary and secondary school there. My civilian life came to an end when I got recruited by guerrillas in 1976.

Truly speaking, I wasn't politically conscious of the things that were happening then. I was very young. What I remember was the fact that our parents would complain of colonialism and terror they underwent in terms of discrimination, underpayment, and beatings because they were black. During that time there was a hype for people joining the liberation struggle and those left behind became a social misfit. Fortunately, in 1976 guerrillas came into our area taking the elderly and youths to join the liberation struggle. We were taken in the afternoon and driven towards the Botswana border. These recruiters were very instructive. It was never easy to leave your parents behind and join the liberation.

By dusk which was around 7pm, we reached the borderline of Zimbabwe and Botswana and this is where we were instructed to crawl underneath the borderline to cross. They told us to move very quickly and cross over. As we were crossing were told never to look back and begin to run in the direction where we got intercepted by another team of recruiters. Those that we had initially, had disappeared to an unknown destination. We reached a certain place in Botswana where we slept, it was in the thick of the bush. This was around midnight. Around 4 am recruiters instructed us to wake up and run in the direction where there was the main road. Already, two lorries were waiting for us to reach our final destination in Francistown.

As energetic as we were, we quickly had to jump into the lorries and we were taken to prison. We slept there I think for three or so days. A lot had changed in terms of our lifestyle. At the prison, we would be asked what we dreamt of the previous night. I do not know the motive why they would ask that. The moment one responded that they dreamt of fighting, flying with the airplane, or anything aligned to the struggle, they were then chosen to go to Zambia. I got pained why I was not dreaming of such, but I later lied to them after three days that I had dreamt of an airplane. Black Swine, Sabhonjwana and I think a guy called Normal were very active during the selection..

The next morning, we were ferried to Zambia and the first destination was at Livingstone. I got excited when I boarded a plane and saw so many lights as this was the first time to experience all such. We moved as a big group as both women and men. In no time we were told to return to the plane. This time we landed at Lusaka airport. I still had the same feeling that I had when I saw lights, cars, and the beauty of Lusaka. Believe me, I had already believed that I was going to live a luxurious life. Some lorries were outside waiting for us too. They were quite big. We were instructed to jump into them. This time recruiters had begun to be so harsh and showing us their other side that we were pursuing war, not luxuries. Some who couldn't climb in were forced in forcefully. My journey to liberation had started. As lorries moved, I lost the sense of direction, I could not make out where we were coming from or heading to. I could not figure out where the north and south were. The lorry was moving so fast in the bush where they were no lights whatsoever. It is then that I discovered that we were pursuing war than luxuries as the situation just changed from good to bad.

We arrived by midnight at a transit camp called Nampundwe. There was so much activity going on there. I remember as we arrived there, we were given food that is isitshwala and beans for we were so much hungry. Imagine the whole journey from Francistown to Livingstone to Nampundwe. The next morning, we were asked to remove our clothes and wear combat regalia that we used to call rice. The regalia was so big, was infested with lice, and had a funny smell. We had to put on the regalia as instructed but it had funny sizes, but you had to wear such and find a way of making it fit. This is the time that we all got new names and I was now called Cecelia Sibanda. That was now my new name. After we had put on our regalia, we were told in a parade that the next morning we were going to meet Joshua Nkomo and welcome him at the Airport. I was very excited that I would finally see Joshua Nkomo.

That very day, we woke up so early and the whistle was blown. Instructors then told us to run to the airport to meet Joshua Nkomo. Little did we know that it was a trick to make us go for a road run. We ran so fast almost 15kms. As we were running some were fainting, vomiting, and some lagging behind. You would reach a point then return as fast as you could. The road run was so difficult I tell you. We assembled at the parade point while we waited for others to join us. As soon as others had returned there was a nearby mountain and we were showed how to climb the mountain using the frog jump tactics, rolling, crawling, and doing another one called number 9. When the time for breakfast came by, we couldn't eat or do anything. None stood up to receive their breakfast.

While we were still nursing confusion and fatigue from the exercises we had done, we were told that every night that we were going to train at Mwembeshi. A selection from our group was made which included men and women. That very night, big lorries came and we were told to board those lorries in numbers. We traveled to Mwembeshi and as soon as we arrived, we pitched up our tents. Women were put on the western side of the camp and men were on the eastern side. This was the day that ushered in my new military life. We were the second group of ladies to train with men after the first group of eight ladies who first trained at Mwembeshi and later moved to Morogoro.

At Mwembeshi we were put in companies. These companies ranged from A up to H. The numbers of women were limited but they strived to make each company have at least six or eight women amongst men. What men did was exactly what we also did. There was no clear distinction as ZPRA was training soldiers and men or women. It was really difficult as instructors would not differentiate whether you are men or women, they trained us as one.

What made the training difficult was the fact that we were not separated that woman should train in isolation from men, no! We trained together. The training included commissariat lessons of the objectives of the war, gun stripping, and assembly, how to use guns, topography, range, the crossing of rivers, bayonet charge, and crossing of obstacles. Our instructors were very harsh and never compromised their standards. I remember Magadlela used to say, 'Sisempini lapha, alibuyanga lapha ukuzohlala kuhle engathi lisemasofeni. Lize ukuzo-trainer nzima.' (This is war, you never came here to sit comfortably on sofas but to train harder.) He was responsible for the bayonet charge. I Magadlela would make you carry a gun in all directions and in the position that he wanted. The guy was so rough.

Other instructors included camp commander Eddie Sigoge. Sigoge was also another character who specialized in obstacle crossing and all. He would fire live bullets when training us so we appreciate what he meant. There was also Stanley Gagisa Nleya who specialized in physic, judo, and exercises. The guy was very fit. He was born a leader. The challenge was that he would insult and not choose a word when he was training. To him, an untrained and not fit soldier was a doko meaning rubbish in the TjiKalanga language but he was later identified as Doko. There was also Philip Valerio Sibanda who was more into combat training and sometimes in commissariat training. PV was always calm but always serious. Other instructors included Moses Phinda, Stanley Doko Gagisa, Arab, Doctor Mbeya, Sibangani, Jockey, Ethan, Ntatshana, and Maphara. Some women instructors included, there was Grace, Bvundzai, Constance, Belinda, and Audrey. We couldn't separate them from men instructors. They inspired us to say the least.

We trained there for six months. I was among a group of eight ladies to be deployed at Victory Camp as security guards. Part of the assignment was to vet people who were going into the camp, provide security to the services as guards, and do all security protocols that included vetting those coming in to stay inside the camp. At that time, I was in possession of an AK47 although there were also men that were in our security department but we're doing anti-air security outside the camp.

I managed to be on-site for quite a long time and when others like Zegeu were assigned further training in intelligence I was now under National Security Organization (NSO, which was a security department headed by Dumiso Dabengwa). While I was at Victory Camp, I was instructed to go to Mkushi Camp to investigate certain reports about infiltration as an NSO officer in disguise. I went there in disguise as an instructor to join the group of fifty women who were chosen from the first group to be instructors although my primary job was to investigate issues of infiltration. It was not easy. While I was still at VC, it was noted from the reports that some of our camps had been infiltrated. In one of the reports, it was noted that at Mkushi there were people who would be seen at night wearing [uniforms?] like ZPRA commanders and in most cases, the camp would have different footprints and unusual shoe prints. The star shoe print was the most popular. I was taken to Mkushi and joined other instructors who were to train the second group of recruits but also to operate as an undercover. After we did our investigation, a lot was discovered and it became apparent that anytime we were going to be bombed. This is not a secret! What was not clear was when was the bombing going to start and which camp was going to be hit first. We had now gathered all the information but then it took a while for the superiors to respond to some of the stories of infiltration.

In no time while I was at Mkushi, we got bombed as shown by the indications from the investigations. I was not aware of the terrain in Mkushi but I ran in the direction of the river and hid. Fortunately, I managed to hit a thicket which then allowed me to see what was happening. A lot of people suffered. Some were shot, others got trapped and couldn't run away. They were dropping Napalm which was burning others alive. It was really difficult. They dropped another bomb in front of me. I had told myself that I was going to die. The bomb failed to go off I think because it fell on a swampy area and it lost traction. In no time I stood up and ran in the direction of the river with my Simonov gun. I ran and managed to cross the river at the shallow end although I was afraid of crocodiles along the way. I ran and after running for close to a kilometer I found a place and decided to sleep there. What worried me the most was the fact that I was new to the place. I did not know their safety zone or where the regrouping zone was since I had only one week. I slept there and only got frightened by a duiker that was just passing by. I then walked up following the swampy area and I got to a nearby homestead and the Zambia national complained and told me that they were not safe to accommodate me. However, they showed me the direction they had seen in their TVs and radios.

We regrouped with others and we were taken, we were then taken to Kafue at a farm that belonged to Milner. At that time, casualties were receiving treatment and those that had been injured were taken abroad to receive treatment. Joshua Nkomo and other command elements came to Kafue. In no time a new camp was opened which was called Solwezi. It was further up close to the Congo-Zambia border post. At Solwezi, we stayed there although we continued with training which wasn't at a large scale as compared to Mkushi. This was the same time when the women's brigade was formed and appointments were made. Gertrude Mpala was appointed the brigade commander while Ossie Mhandu became the deputy. We stayed there until the time of the ceasefire when we returned home. I was not demobilized but was attested into the army.

CHAPTER 7

'As we were trained, we saw no difference between women and male instructors.'

Doreen Mathe

(Mwembeshi trained cadre)

Fig 17: Freedom fighter, Doreen Mathe, who was trained at Mwembeshi. She was deployed as a security officer responsible for vetting protocols in Victory Camp and later received further security training in East Germany. She was attested into the then newly formed Zimbabwe National Army under the military police department.

The name that I was given by my father and mother was Sebenzile Ncube. However, my war name became Doreen Mathe. Born in the 1960s, I grew up in Plumtree in a village called Tjehanga. I did my primary level up to grade seven but shortly when I was about to proceed to secondary level, I then decided to join the liberation struggle which was in 1976. It was in December when schools had closed after we had organized ourselves to join the liberation struggle. We were sixty-six in total, thirty-three boys and thirty-three girls. Organizing ourselves into such a group meant that we understood the type of oppression that we sought to correct through joining the liberation struggle. I remember my mother would complain about my behaviour that I needed not to be political as this would result in the burning of our homestead by the colonial regime.

But well, how could I have avoided political conscientization when I heard Jane Ngwenya broadcasting and requesting us to join the liberation struggle. I would sneak out at home and listen to Jane with other kids in those homesteads where their parents allowed them to listen to her. Jane was quite a character that we would forever cherish. When she spoke you would get all the emotions of anger from what she said about the nature of oppression, laugh because of how she dramatized her call, and ultimately wish to join the liberation struggle.

More so, we would hear our parents and teachers talking openly about Joshua Nkomo who was to them the supposed messiah to bring an end to the regime, and hence he needed us as his manpower. I couldn't resist the temptation of joining the liberation struggle. Besides, it was now fashionable to join the struggle and you would be considered otherwise if you were left behind especially in my area. My first experience with the guerrillas was when my mother has sent me to Plumtree town to buy groceries using the Shu-shine bus service. I bought the grocery and I packed it into a medium-sized cardboard box and carried it on top of my head.

On my way back home after I had crossed the river, I heard someone saying, '*ps... ps... ps.*' When I looked back to see who was calling me, I saw no one. They repeated this twice and I was not seeing anyone. I then proceeded with my walk. When I approached a big tree, two men approached from the front and the other two at the back and that time I was in the middle I couldn't run away.

At first, I didn't know the fact that they were guerrillas. They greeted me and asked where I had gone and for what reason. I told them that I had been sent to buy groceries by my mother at Plumtree. Their major question was which mode of transport I had used. I told them that I had used Shu-shine and one of them said, 'eish.' They became inquisitive of how far it had gone and approximately how many minutes. I think they wanted to make money from the bus as they used to do or in some instances, they would recruit from the buses.

When I thought they had finished their interrogation, they began to ask whether I had listened to any radio program before and whether was I aware of, *amalw'ecatsha, amagandanga or amaguerilla*. I responded by saying I listen to radio Zambia, have heard Jane speak and I am aware of Nkomo and his guerrillas. These guerrillas responded by saying that I was lucky to have finally met the amalw'ecatsha in person! I then said it was okay. They began to request what was inside the box and of which they wanted the grocery. I then explained that I couldn't give them the grocery as I feared my mother. I was now scared whether they might snatch the box and run away. I then gave them a packet of biscuits and they laughed and allowed me to go.

When I had taken about four steps, they stopped me and asked me how I will respond in case I would be asked by Rhodesian forces who had stopped me on my way. With the little knowledge of what we were told by our parents, I then said I would tell the forces that I was stopped by other community members who were looking for their cattle. They laughed and allowed me to go. I took five steps and they stopped me once more. They asked me whether I was going to tell my parents at home and I said yes. They all said do not as your mother will go on to tell their neighbour and such will reach to the colonial regime, hence I will have my home burnt down. They went on to ask where I stayed and had to describe and show them my homestead. When I reached home, I was now stressed whether I said the right thing to them or what if they come and burn my homestead. The fact that they told me not to divulge any information to anyone troubled me as I wanted to share such a scenario with my mother. I went straight to sleep at 7pm but I could see that my mother realized that there was something that was bothering me.

After two weeks when my mother had gone out to the fields in the afternoon and I was with my young sister, five guerrillas came to our homestead. They were carrying guns. This frightened me. They told me that they wanted something to eat as they were tired and hungry. Surprisingly, out of five, I recognized three of them that had stopped me when I was coming from Plumtree. I then asked them to go into the hut. They went straight into the hut. When my mother came … from the field, we told her that there were visitors and she said I [should] give them food and we cooked. While we were serving them, they were telling us that they had taken money from the shops, rural council offices, and buses. The other one had to stand up while eating and showed us the type of cigarette that they were smoking. The man had to say the type of cigarettes they smoked was only found in South Africa, Botswana, and Zambia and if the regime finds those in the yard we would be beaten even if we deny for, they know the type of people going around with it. Still, on that, they made it clear that their shoe prints were known so the best was to sweep the yard after they leave and burn all their cigarettes. I am telling you this so that you understand that we did all these roles long before we had to train militarily.

It was around 6pm when we started our journey. I was with my uncle and his cousin. I had to tell my mother I was going to the liberation struggle that very night. She only responded by saying I was not serious and insane. My grandfather had to intervene with my mother to give me the blessings to join the liberation struggle. Because, we had arranged with other youngsters, to meet at 8pm at a certain point to begin the journey. We left and began our journey. We crossed Thekwane river, proceeded to Dombodema and we were making noise. At Dombodema we saw flares that were thrown in the air to light up the area. These guerrillas that were going with us had to quickly instruct us to sit down and remain quiet as they had seen that the Rhodesians were close by. We proceeded for an hour and we reached the border and guerrillas told us that we had reached a very dangerous zone but we managed to cross the fence to Botswana.

We continued walking and we had only to put up there. We never slept but talked all night. Early morning, we began to walk and crossed a certain river. Where we were, it was as if we were on top of a mountain and we heard the guerrillas talk saying that there is Vasco with another group. Indeed, we saw another group coming in our direction. It was a group that took kids from the Mphini Ndiweni area-an area where Dorcas Ndiweni a military instructor who trained recruits at Mkushi hails from, but we were from Tjehanga. We were then combined into a single group. We were given food and got fed. In no time vehicles came by and took us to a police station called Tsetsebe. We stayed there for a while and lorries came by [and] took us to Francistown prison where we slept.

The next morning, we were taken to the camp which had a lot of people who also intended to join the liberation struggle. There were many people both boys and girls. We never stayed long at Francistown. Our stay was only two. There is a guy who was called Sabhonjwana who used to address us. We were flown to Zambia, arrived at Livingstone before it reached the final destination at Lusaka. At Lusaka airport, it is then that we got addressed by Nikita Mangena. I think he had not come to address us but on some other business but had to talk to us as he had been requested by the command element to speak as a sign of respect. I am sure he was flying out of the country. Lorries came by and we were taken to a transit camp called Nampundwe. We arrived there around 9pm together with our male counterparts.

Early morning at Nampundwe, I heard people making war cries and singing. It was scary especially when you are not used to the type of military life. There were doing road runs and toyi-toyi of those that were now guerrillas. It was not a training camp. On the third day of our stay, we were told to join the road run and other military drills. As we were training a senior guerrilla called Cephas Cele came to the camp from Lusaka. He found us doing drills while wearing our dresses. There was a drill which was called number 6 and one was left almost exposed I mean naked if they had worn a dress. Cele found us doing it in dresses and he was so cross to those guerrillas for allowing us to do Number 6 while in dresses. He did not hide his anger and asked them how they felt seeing us in such a state all in the name of training. We got dismissed there and there. He then instructed that the next day lorries were coming to ferry recruits for training at Mwembeshi. The next day, we travelled to Mwembeshi. We arrived when others were at the parade square being dismissed to have their dinner. We had to join them, we ate and we were only shown where we were supposed to sleep.

The next morning while at the parade quiet as it was, a tall man came through, and those that had been addressing us stopped talking as he was passing by. The man said, '*Liyangikhangela kanti lina bodaki lingifanisa lobani.*' (Why are recruits all staring at me as if I look familiar to them). We thought maybe he was going to address us but he passed his comment and drifted away. His name was Eddie Sigoge and he was the camp commander. When he had passed by, instructors had to put us into companies. Shortly, before the training, Jason Moyo came to address us of the objectives of the struggle. Unfortunately, days or so after he had addressed us, we were told by the camp commander that JZ Moyo had died. Sigoge addressed us for an hour about JZ and we noticed that Sigoge was getting emotional about the death of JZ. I was among the group of recruits who were chosen to attend the funeral of JZ at Lusaka.

Our training was a military-type that was aligned to guerrilla warfare. We did a lot of road runs, drills, explosives, gun assembly, judo, and tactics. Sigoge was responsible for obstacle training and he would fire live bullets in the midst of trying to come out from the obstacle. He was teaching land mines and explosives. You would crawl under the wire to come out of the obstacle while he was firing live bullets. This was done to get acquainted with live bullets as we trained using sticks. Sigoge also trained us in judo. Imagine he was very tall but would do a forward fall as if he was short. He would demonstrate and would require one to do as he did. Grace Muchachi was also good at judo. She was very good. I remember the first time we saw her doing all the tricks, male recruits marvelled. Muchachi was very good at what she was doing. This speaks to the fact that ZPRA had indeed trained soldiers.

There was also Stanley Gagisa who was responsible for military drills. He was emotional and would not take nonsense. He would revert to speaking in TjiKalanga if you did what he never wanted. He would say, One two doko! If he called you Doko he meant that you were a rubbish soldier not fit for anything but he was later called Doko as his nickname. Philip Valerio Sibanda was also another instructor. He was always quiet and soft-spoken. PV has always been quiet and very professional. He was very different to other instructors as he would not share jokes, laugh or pass any jovial remarks. He meant business. I'm not saying others were not but he had his unique way. He specialized in combat fighting, tactic training, and topography.

There were many other instructors like Jack Mpofu, Grey, Rueben, Mamba, Magadlela (affectionately known as Thambolenyoka) who did bayonet charge training, and Billy Mzamo. Magadlela specialized in bayonet charge training and was very charismatic. He would jump, skirmish and would make remarks that made us laugh. Lessons on the commissariat were taught by Emmanuel and Khwela Chitambo. Among the female instructors, there were Grace Muchachi and Bvundzai Tawona. They were good and blended well with the male instructors. We saw no difference between them and other male instructors. What made it good was the fact that in the absence of any other male instructor the two would take over and train even harder than the male instructors themselves. Grace could jump and spin in the air. Sigoge would ask her to demonstrate to us. He was very proud of Grace. Bvundzai was responsible for artillery training. Stripping a gun and assembling it. Those ladies were exceptionally good.

After the training, I was posted to Victory Camp as security personnel responsible for vetting anyone coming into the camp and also providing security. I worked with Dorcas, Samkeliso, Cecelia, Audrey and Jane Ndlovu (Morogoro). We were working closely with Mazinyane vetting anyone coming and going out of the camp. I remember my name was also called out as one of the instructors to go and train recruits at Mkushi. However, I got very late as I was still at the river when others were preparing to go. I only found the vehicles gone. I was told to remain in the security department. The next time I was called by Cecil who was the camp commander as they needed security personnel for close-up presidential security. I was sent to the State House at Lusaka to provide such security to Nkomo together with others.

I was further sent for advanced security training in then East Germany, remember that time there was Cold War. I remember there was Nxele, Siphelile who is still a police officer, Juliet, Tiny, Jonathan, Nathan, Mandaza, and I. We did that course for eight months specializing in close security. Those instructors were very tough as we were taught the tactics of security combining it with intelligence. It was a course worth the cause. All the bombardment happened when I was in East Germany. We saw all the news broadcast on television. This was very bad. Upon completing the training, I resumed my security work at Nkomo's place still under the close-up security at Woodlands after spending a month at Kafue training camp. I also stayed with secretaries to Ackim Ndlovu as their security. However, I was later moved to stay with Getrude Mpala who was the women brigade commander, and Sithabile Muchachi who was the chief of training for the brigade. However, Muchachi later moved to the UK and Chipo Daughters Mabuwa took over the responsibility.

At that time, I switched the role into a military intelligence unit. Remember, I was doing a security role for civilian leaders under the banner of NSO led by Dabengwa, Swazini and I think Bhutshe but because I was now transferred into the camp, I was now working in the military intelligence. I worked under the commands of Patrick Mhandu (affectionaely known as *sekuru*[10]) who later became the husband to Ossie Olie Mhandu. Mhandu was my boss. This was now on the eve of independence. I came back home with others and because I had lost my father in 1978, I went home to Plumtree and so I did not go to Sierra Assembly point. I joined others who were at Castle Arms in Richmond, Bulawayo. I only stayed for a night or two. I proceeded to Windemere along Umguza where there was another group of women who were there. I remember there was Siyabonga Kaunda, Ingrid, and others who had done police servicing courses at Lilayi in Zambia. I was attested at Brady barracks under military police and retired in that department. I got married to my former military instructor the late Eddie Sigoge Mlotshwa and we had four children and grandchildren as well.

Fig 18: Doreen holding a gun at Nkomo's residence in Lusaka.. **Picture source**: Accessed from Doreen's personal archive.

[10]In Shona language, the word sekuru means either grandfather or uncle. Mhandu was nicknamed sekuru as he was a bit older than most of his contemporaries and was known for his skills in baking bread. Mhandu trained with former VP Kembo Mohadi, Busobenyoka, Blackswine, and Captain Nyathi.

PICTURES OF VICTORY CAMP

Pictures used in this publication were accessed from the Zenzo Nkobi Collection kept at Mafela Trust and the South African History Archive (SAHA).

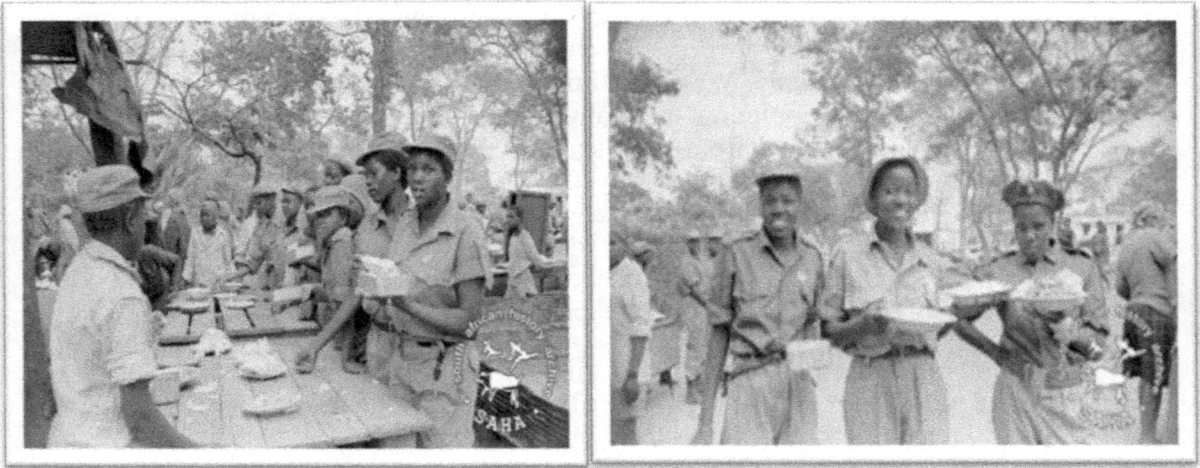

Fig 19 and Fig 20 : Women combatants having a meal in Victory Camp

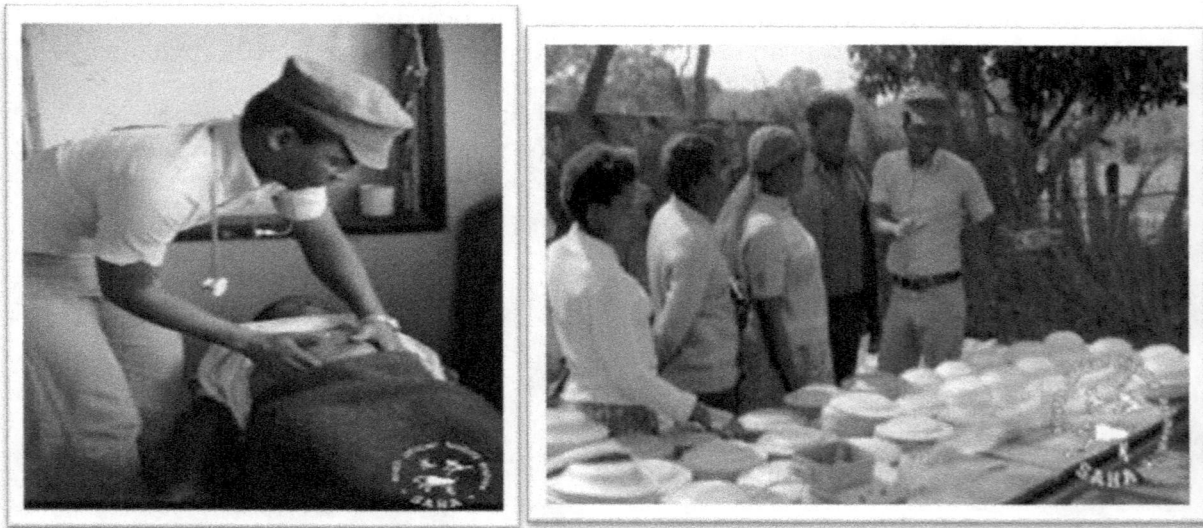

Fig 21: Health official, Dr Bango examining a pregnant woman at Victory Camp. Women who were found pregnant within the training phase were withdrawn from training and sent back to Victory Camp.

Fig 22: Food inspection at Victory Camp.

CHAPTER 8

'Our journey to the liberation struggle was different and so was our destiny'

Siyabonga Kaunda
(Mkushi trained cadre)

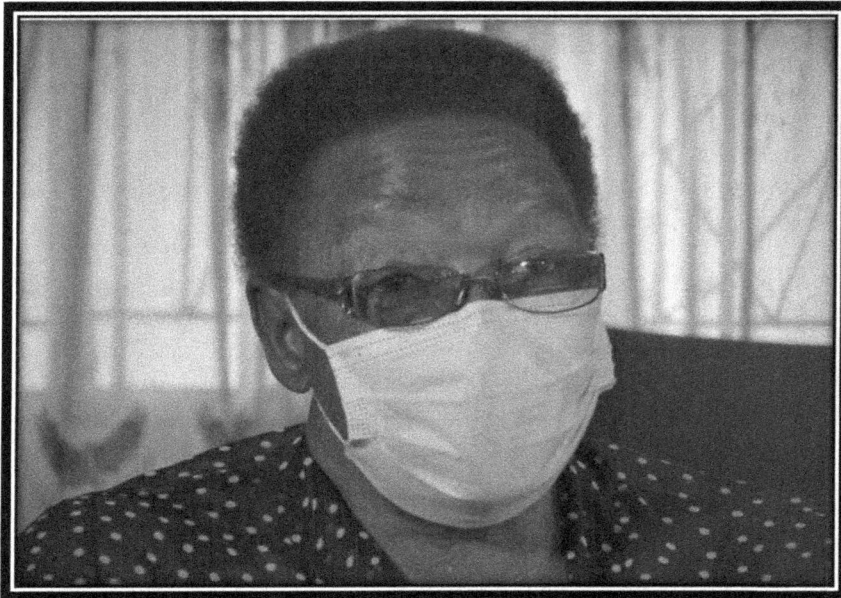

Fig 23: Freedom Fighter, Siyabonga Kaunda, who was trained at Mkushi and went for further police training at Lilayi in Lusaka. In 1980 she was integrated into the then newly formed Zimbabwe National Army.

My name is Jacqueline Mathwasa and [I] got the surname Nkala after I got married post-independence. My war name was Siyabonga Kaunda. I went to the war in 1977. I was among the first group of female cadres to be trained at Mkushi. I come from Gwanda district from Matshetsheni under Mzimuni at a village called Singungwe. However, I grew up in Bulawayo in Babourfields suburb. I did my primary school in Bulawayo and the secondary up to Form 2. When I failed Form 2, I was sent to stay and help my maternal uncle at his shop in Matobo district at a village called Silobini. The idea was to correspond and supplement my studies while working at his shop.

In 1977, I went to Silobini where I worked as a shopkeeper selling goods in one of the shops belonging to my uncle who was called Deloli Moyo, while also corresponding. I must say my uncle was a renowned businessman who owned a bus company called Godlwayo and had a lot of shops, butchery, and bottle stores.

The butchery used to slaughter cows for sale every Tuesday. I liked beef a lot and I made it a point to be available when they slaughtered as I knew I would eat more meat and enjoy it. This other Tuesday the guy who works at the butchery did likewise and invited me to come over as the meat was now ready. And as per the routine, I went to the butchery which was at the back of the shop. While I was at the corner of the shop approaching the butchery, I saw a man carrying a gun. I got scared and the man only gave me a sign to keep quiet and only said, '*sh... sh... sh!*' I stood there and I was very afraid. The man told me to go back to the shop and I complied. He then followed me into the shop that I worked in and I realized that others like that man had also gone to the nearby shops, bottle stores, and butcheries. While he was at the shop the other man joined him in the shop where I worked. In the shop they began to loot, taking all the goods that were on the shelves like food, beer, and clothes.

They then moved closer to where I was standing and demanded to know where the safe was and said they wanted all the money. I showed them and they took it into one of their bags but later gave me back to keep for later use. Those two that had appeared to me at first, disappeared and the other one appeared from nowhere. This time all those who were held hostage like me in other shops were now all assembled in the shop that I worked in. The man told us that at 5pm someone was going to come and take us to an unknown destination. There was quite a number adults and young people. I think there were only five of us young people. We complied and listened because when you are dealing with an armed individual while you are defenceless you just comply.

Indeed, the said guy came at 5pm together with the other three guys. This time they had come to collect us, they went and took the messenger to the chief and the local Agritex officer who worked with local farmers, and they were killed in the shop while we were watching. They began to tell us that they were ZAPU-ZPRA guerrillas who were commanded by Joshua Nkomo, who was on a mission to liberate the country. They took us that time at night and we also got mixed with others that were recruited in the local council bar. Our journey to the liberation struggle had just begun. We began to walk, climb mountains and we slept along the main road. I think they had organized a bus that was to ferry us early morning to the unknown destination. Indeed, early morning a bus came through and we were all instructed to board. We were all dropped in areas at Kezi, at a homestead that belonged to one of the village heads. At that time, we had remained with three recruiters and others were nowhere to be found. One of them began to call me the daughter of *Bhuzha*,[11] I still have no clue what that means. They reminded me to keep the money that they made me take from the

---

[11] Bhuzha was a popular word in the mid 1970's which often referred to anyone who had wealthy parents.

safe place at the shop. We went a long way still walking and we arrived at a local chief near Shashi River. I wish I would narrate the incidents of the things that other recruits and I, especially girls, went through. Truly, speaking such things bring pain to me as I still consider them an ordeal. I wish I could narrate that but well you can use your imagination of the things that happened especially for a girl child. At that time, we were now ten of usfemale recruits.

We arrived close by the homestead of the chief, we were made to wait by the bush, and it is them that proceeded to see the chief. After some deliberations with the chief, they came to collect us at night and went into the homestead of the chief. They took us in, we ate, and we were allowed to have a bath. We spent two days in that homestead. I do not know where the recruiters were staying during the two days. They only came checking on us and giving us information that we couldn't proceed as police officers were on patrol. However, on the third day, they came at night and told us that we are proceeding with our journey. We proceeded, one of them led the way and the other was following behind us making sure we do not run away.

When we had crossed over to the other side of Shashi River, while at the bank I was ordered to handover the bag of money that they had made me keep. I handed over the money and they began to give us more instructions. They told us not to either look back or think of returning. They made it clear that they had done their duty and there were chances that they might or might not see them. They gave us the direction that we needed to follow up to the nearby homestead and if we got lost, we needed to ask people to show us the way and also tell them that we wanted to join the liberation struggle to Zambia. As they were returning to the other side of the bank, they pointed their gun upwards and shot twice. This was the first time I heard a gunshot and they disappeared.

As instructed, we proceeded and asked the nearby homestead and they told us that several people had recently left for Gobajango. We followed the said direction and arrived at Gobajango where we found several people that had involuntarily or voluntarily recruited like us. There was a mix of the young and the elderly. We stayed at least a day and a big truck came by and took us to Selibe-Phikwe. Selibe-Phikwe was a prison where nearly every recruit stayed with prisoners. We stayed at cells. We stayed a month while groups that had arrived before us were taken in turns to Zambia. Sadly, you can imagine that I had not come with clothes. The only clothes I had were those that I had put on. Our day also came when we were taken to Zambia. We were all happy when we were taken to a big plane. Our aspirations were that we were going to have a better life after seeing the plane. Little did we know of the hardships that we were likely to be confronted with. Our plane landed behind the airport and not at the usual drive-through but behind the main entrance. After we landed a big truck was already outside waiting to ferry us to the next destination. That time it was almost very dark around 8pm. I then sensed that what we hoped for was never going to come through, as signs of challenges ahead were all over.

We arrived at Victory Camp, in the middle of the night. On our arrival, we were given food, that was sadza and relish which was almost sugar beans but it was not beans. It was *umtshatshatsha*. I couldn't eat because I was not used to that relish. I only ate sadza and drank water. After that, we were directed to a big hall where we were told that we would sleep. The hall was called Big Bhawa as it was roomy and nearly accommodated everyone. As such, we were given three blankets, as we slept in the middle of the night those that considered themselves seniors of the place came and stole our blankets and we woke up without. What they used to do was that they took new blankets from the newcomers only to abandon the old ones as they now had lice. It wasn't nice at all. Lice would come and make you feel uncomfortable. But with time we got used to them. By the way, we used to call lice comrade for it then became part and parcel of our lifestyle. We woke up the next morning and there was an instruction that all those who had come the previous day needed to register. During the registration process, I was given the name Siyabonga Kaunda.

At Victory Camp, we would wake up early around 5am to do what was called toyi-toyi. It was a type of physical training that made one run, chant a war cry, and carry out various demonstrations as per the instructor. We also did lessons on the objective of the war and a bit of gun assembly. Instructors were females that had trained in Morogoro. I remember there was Grace Mutshatshi, Bvundzai Tawona,[12] and the other one who we used to call her Gumbi. There were no male instructors because Victory Camp was only a transit camp that had young kids, boys, girls, and women. I couldn't eat because of the type of food that was available. I just couldn't eat.

Resultantly, I became so thin and got so ill. I was taken to the nearby hospital at Lusaka which was called VTH. I stayed there for nearly one and a half months. When they discharged me that morning, the nurse told me that my family, alluding to those from Victory camp, were on their way to pick me up. I had to ask the nurse how far was it for one to move from the hospital to reach Victoria Falls. The nurse was puzzled and asked me why I needed to know the kilometres and the direction and I responded to her that I needed to go back home as I was not coping. While at the hospital, I had this great feeling that we were very close to Victoria Falls. They came and picked me up as I had nothing I could do to stop them from coming or running away. I had a terrible feeling of regret. I thought of the harassment I got from the lice at night, the type of food, and the general training setup. I only got used to the lifestyle after some time but, well, it was not easy.

After coming from the hospital, I stayed another two months or so and instruction came that some from our group were due for training. We were then called for a parade where some people were chosen for training based on fitness. I had two of my friends one called Grace Dube and the other one called

---

[12] Grace Muchachi and Bvundzai Tawona were among the first group of nine female combatants to receive ZPRA's military training. Refer to their full profile and interview which are also included in this publication.

Sithembewena. During the process of choosing, there was a senior ZPRA officer who was called Cephas Cele[13]. He was the one responsible for qualifying one to go training. Both my friends were chosen and I was left out by Cele who argued that I wasn't fit, I was going to die during the training. I felt the pain of being left out now that my close friends were going. Sithembewena told me to drift away from those that were left out as she had a plan of dragging me to those that were chosen for training.

The two of them sandwiched me between them and I found myself on the other side registering with them as someone due for training. Indeed, their plan worked. The following day, my name was called once more with those that were meant to go for the training. I went to train as a soldier because of the bravery of the two of my friends who sacrificed for me. We travelled at night to Mkushi and arrived at midnight. Mkushi was a thick forest. We slept at night and woke up early morning. That morning we began to pitch up tents and we were put in various companies which we maintained in all our training and any other eating, staying arrangement at the camp. We would wake up around 5 am, go for a parade, and be dismissed for a toyi-toyi. We would run a kilometres and a half or at times more.

We were also given sticks with a sling which was to mimic a gun. As a trainee, you were supposed to carry that stick with you and never to lose it. Later in the training we were given real guns that we used for gun assembly, and bayonet charge. We would be made to carry an AK-47 with hands raised for 15 minutes. Part of our training included the commissariat lessons which emphasized the reasons why we joined the liberation struggle. The emphasis was that the white man took everything from us, the black, and we were to reclaim our identity and resources with the white man. We were not taught to hate the white man but to fight the system of discrimination and to reform the system so that we coexist with them in harmony. Lessons were never about racism or teaching how to hate the whites. Through the lessons, we ended up seeing that indeed the whites took control of everything. Instructors constituted six males that came from Somalia. I only remember three that is Kumbirai, Sotsha, and Mananavira. Then there was also our camp commander who was Phinda, there was Ntatshana, and the logistics man who was Makanyanga.

When we were due for a pass-out after six months, we delayed a bit as we were told that Joshua Nkomo was held up on other programs. A group of 50 females from our group were chosen to be instructors of the next group of females that were moved from VC like us. I was not chosen to be an instructor. The chosen group of 50 remained behind as we moved to establish a new camp, New Mkushi, which was about 2km from the old base. We were moved from the old

---

[13]Cephas Cele was ZPRA's Chief of personnel and manpower. He assumed the office when the late Abraham Nkiwane was deployed to another assignment. At this point, Cele was responsible for the selection of recruits for training, further training and deployment.

base to accommodate the recruits who were about to come and train. These are the recruits that were bombed. I moved to the new site with others as we were waiting to be deployed.

At New Mkushi we would wake up early morning for exercises, parade, and wait for some orders or assignments. At first, we would just do the daily morning routine and spend the whole day seated. Daily new orders would come as others would be chosen and deployed for further training to be teachers, nurses, and sent abroad for military training.

Our day came when Sifoto, Christabel, Keznet and I were chosen for further training at Lilayi Police in Zambia. Before we were moved to Lilayi, we were taken back to VC and stayed there a few days. On our way to Lilayi, we were taken to Joshua Nkomo's residence. They presented us before him that these are the girls that have been chosen for further training as police cadets. Police cadet training meant that after one completed the course, one would be elevated to a position of station commander. After a month when we were still at Lilayi, a group of thirty girls also came but were doing further training of a police course which had an opening rank of constable. It was more different from ours. We did the course and completed it after 6 months. Still, on that, I have to state that when Freedom Camp and Mkushi got bombed I was still at Lilayi.

We saw them heading in the direction of FC first and we were later told that Mkushi had been rounded up. An order was made that as cadets we were supposed to go to the hospital where casualties were to donate blood to those who needed it. I had heard that my brother was now at FC and when I heard that they had bombed FC I thought of my brother. The same was true when I got to the hospital to donate blood, I had told myself that my brother was supposed to benefit from my blood. I was only told that that very morning before the bombing, he had travelled to the Soviet Union for further training. I was not there but I know and I can assertively say major casualties came from the recruits as they had recently joined. It was terrible.

After police training, we went back to VC and Nkomo made an order that the trained were to be deployed elsewhere not in the transit camp. We were then taken to Solwezi which was at Zambia near the then Zaire (DRC) border. The trained personnel that was bombed at Mkushi also came in and stayed with us. The four of us who had trained at Lilayi we were called once more for further training in Yugoslavia about advanced police studies. After training, we came back to Solwezi but we were then deployed to various ports. I was deployed at Zimbabwe House which was the headquarters of ZAPU-ZPRA. I worked there as a typist.

During the 1980 elections, we voted at Victoria Falls although we lost. Some were already in Zimbabwe but we remained in Zambia. I came back with other female trained personnel and we went to Sierra Assembly point in Gweru where all trained females were accommodated for the Demobilization Demilitarization

Reintegration (DDR). This was a time when they would choose those that they wanted and those left out in the integration were requested to go back home. I was chosen on board and finally integrated at One Brigade as an ordinary soldier. Later I was deployed to the military police department. That is when I started policing affairs in my country as a policewoman. I then went to a selection board where promotions are made, I became successful. I passed through all the stages and retired from the army as Lieutenant Colonel. In 1983, I got married to Lincoln Nkala who was the son of a Zapu nationalist Lazarus Nkala.

CHAPTER 9

'After all, we ran a good race'

Simangaliso Mpofu
(Mkushi trained cadre and survivor of the bombardment)

Fig 24: Freedom Fighter, Simangaliso Mpofu, who was trained at Mkushi. She is a survivor of the Mkushi bombing and later received further training in intelligence and counterintelligence training in Yugoslavia. In 1980 she was integrated into the Zimbabwe National Army.

My name is Queen - Elizabeth Diketso Dube. I was born at Gwanda at Mapate in an area called Matulungundu. I grew up staying with my aunt and uncle. These are the two people that brought me up together with the other two sisters of mine. I went to war when I was thirteen years old. This was in 1977. I went to Gungwe and Mapate schools. The journey of going to the war started when I was doing my daily routine with my sisters. This was when we were herding livestock in the bush together with other community children. At the time, I was no longer going to school as my parents had stopped me from going to school as there were rumours that there were people called *'amalw'ecatsha'*[14] who were kidnapping,

---

[14]This was a rumor for those days, when young people were leaving for the war and being recruited from schools, and parents may not have known what happened to them.

raping, and torturing children. I had stopped going to school as my parents feared the worst especially rape.

While herding livestock, talks of going to the war among my peers had already gathered momentum. Each day, when we were herding livestock, talks of such nature intensified as this was at the height of the war. One day when we were herding our livestock, three sisters of mine who I stayed with at home decided that they were joining the struggle to fight. Believe me, I didn't know whatever they were alluding to, fighting Smith, and joining Joshua Nkomo. I was very young, but I merely wanted to go because this is what my sisters wanted. That very day, they told me that we are going to the war.

One reason why they took me with them was that they did not want me to return home and begin telling our parents where they had gone to the war. This is the reason why I was dragged in and joined the war. I was co-opted in and went to the struggle as four of us. My sisters were inspired by the teaching of our parents that there was a need for them to join others to go to the struggle. Such thinking was perhaps inspired by the fact that other children from some households had gone and it had become fashionable for a family to send their children to war. Remember political consciousness of the people and especially of Joshua Nkomo increased. Already in the area, [there was] knowledge that a country should be fought for to realize emancipation of the people. In our community, it became popular to say that, *relwela boipuso*, (going to fight for freedom).

It became so popular that naturally, children decided to join the war. But on my part, I used to hear all those stories but it couldn't make any sense at [all] because I was too young. What I knew was that whatever my sisters wanted I followed. No wonder I was able to join them in the struggle. I was thirteen years. Little did I know that I was going to train, fight and become a soldier at the end of the day.

I wanted to go to the war but I never knew what it all entailed. They had told me not to tell anyone as to where we were going required me to keep low and not to tell anyone. My sisters feared that if I stayed behind, they would be exposed, that my aunt would want to know where they had gone and I would have said it as it was. My sisters told me to take one of the beautiful dresses that I had worn at the last Christmas celebration. However, I failed to take it along as my aunt was watching my moves on the eve of our departure. Worse still, I travelled barefooted to Botswana.

The journey had started, I was following what they were saying, and I mean my sisters. We went to cross Shashi River to cross over to Botswana. That time the river was almost full to the brim. One of my sisters crossed over alone. I managed to cross with the other two who were holding me while teaching me to cross the river dragging my feet in the sand so that I don't lose balance and traction.

We managed to cross and when we crossed over, we began to ululate and began to sing in celebration of crossing the river. When we got there, our first stop was at Mtabeng. The responsible people at Mtabeng took us to Gobajango where we were taken to the *kgosi* like a traditional leader or chief who welcomed us. The *kgosi* (local chief) instructed the responsible to take us to Selibe-Phikwe Prison where all recruits were taken to. Thus, we stayed for almost a week before we were taken to Francistown.

Life began to change at Selibe-Phikwe Prison where we used to stay the whole day in the cells. We used to stay in the barracks with prisoners eating a popular food called '*Stampa*'[15]. My life changed drastically and I did not enjoy or like at all. But I had no choice. I had taken that route already. I did not have any regrets about my choices but I found the change depressing. I was young.

We were later moved to Francistown. We stayed in the barracks for quite some time. There was no training. The new setting appeared much better as we began to meet other female recruits there who were taken from Manama school. It became clearer to me that I needed to grow up and become responsible and not rely on the fact that I had sisters. I realized that since I had my sisters I was supposed to be mature as military-level training knew no relative or sister. This was a painful truth hence I needed to adapt and qualify to the new lifestyle. Where there was the scramble for food, I needed to be there and not wait for anyone to do that for me. I'm not saying there was any scramble, it's just an example of what it was to be.

At Francistown, there was a lady who was responsible for the recruits. But mostly the command of the camp was male-dominated but I no longer remember their names. We stayed at a house within the camp which was like a dormitory with bunk beds as we stayed as girls. Food was well cooked where there was tinned fish which was mostly supplied by the Russians. The kind of fish had a lot of oil. We used to bathe, eat, share stories, and sleep. There was no military training at Francistown, neither did we receive any lessons. We just repeated this daily as I have narrated.

A week or so [later] we were taken to Zambia at a place called Victory Camp. When we arrived at Zambia airport and saw the glittering lights of the city of Lusaka, we thought maybe life has changed for the best for us as we kept admiring the splendour and beauty of the city. In no time, vehicles came and took us to Victory Camp.

VC was a transit camp away from the city life where everyone or recruits were taken to the camp. We managed to stay there at VC from February up to September 1977. While it was a transit camp, it was also a training camp, unlike Francistown. We got our first training there. We used to go out for some toyi-

---

[15] Stampa was the type of food which was eaten by recruits and inmates while in the prison cells.

toyi, drills, exercises, bayonet charge. We did all the training. There is nothing we did at Mkushi that we did not do at VC. We had lessons on topography, commissariat, gun assembly and stripping, shooting drills and aiming, etc. Lessons at VC were loaded.

While at VC I remember some male instructors and commanders who were present. There was Cecil, Makanyanga, Sylvester, and Theodophilus among others. Later we were joined by trained female instructors who had trained in Morogoro like Bvundzai Tawona, Grace Mutshatshi[16], Jane, Alice, Belinda, Audrey, and the other Alice, who we used to call her 'shorty'. These I remember very well because they trained us together with the male instructors. Still, at VC another group of trained female instructors from Mwembeshi was deployed [to] train us although we were almost about to leave VC to Mkushi. These instructors included Ingrid, Sakhile, Sithandekile, and Phathi. The two groups of trained females collaborated to inspire and instil discipline in us. However, when we moved to Mkushi female instructors like Jane, Alice, Sithandekile, Audrey joined us and were elevated and became company commanders of our time.

Female instructors trained us so well exactly like our male instructors. I for one never saw the difference between them and the male instructors. They emphasized discipline. They trained us in physical training and how to withstand or overcome the fear to be brave to have endurance.

We were taken to Mkushi Camp which was the only exclusive female training camp. I was in the first group of recruits to be taken there at Mkushi. We trained at Mkushi from 1977 to 1978. When we had completed the training, we moved to another camp called New Mkushi paving [the] way for the second group to be trained. In this new camp, which was called New Mkushi, this is where we were bombed.

At Mkushi there was no joy, it was a military training camp. It was designed in such a way that it should be difficult and match with the standard training of other camps. We would go for days without food, not that it was part of the training but because the terrain made it impossible for lorries delivering food to reach the camp as it was sandy, worse off when it rained cats and dogs. Mkushi area received more rains and you can imagine an area that received a lot of rain with a sandy terrain. At times we would hear that the lorries got stuck in the mud and we would intercept them, thus walking 50km plus or minus to collect foodstuffs that would be brought by the vehicles. I would carry 50kg and walk a wide distance and later someone who would have been paired with me takes over and finishes her portion. This was not very easy.

I found physical training more of a challenge to me as it was demanding and

---

[16]Cited female cadres were the first group of nine female combatants to receive ZPRA's military training. Bvundzai Tawona and Grace Muchachi have their full profile and interview which is included in this publication

draining. I had no problems with other training but military drills, long and short marches, etc. was a struggle. Instructors would not care whether male or women, they would make you do what they requested you to do. This was standard as ZPRA soldiers were to undergo the same training. We would walk 50kms depending on the instructors and run the distance while carrying a bag with 50kgs or anything while having a small bottle of water. This was the type of physical, but well we went through it.

I won't forget one of the male instructors who was called Castro. He was rough and he beat me at one point and almost left me in a death state. I was beaten. He was trained in Somalia. Other instructors included Castro, Amos, Kumbirai, Theodophilus, Makanyanga. There are two whose names I cannot remember, one was responsible for logistics and the other was Kalanga instructor and used to insult others a lot. There was also our camp commander Billy Mzamo, and other female instructors Phinda, Sithandekile, Jane, and Ingrid among others.

Each instructor had their subject which they specialized within delivering lessons using our companies. For example, there were lessons for topography which was for map reading, physical fitness, bayonet, logistics which are today known as stores. If you look at the lessons we were taught, some lessons are now taught at schools. These are the lessons that were taught. Commissariat was purely history and political lessons that taught us the party ideology which was hinged on Marxism and Leninism. We had instructors that were very sharp in delivering such lessons. Therefore, each had something to do, there was no time where an instructor will be found seated without anything to do. Companies exchanged instructors depending on the lesson of the day. Those who were on duty in the kitchen would meet with their quartermaster at the kitchen while cooking. A lot of military tactics would be instilled, e.g., time management, discipline, and alertness.

The teachings connected with … the rest of what was happening. Because I was young and did not see it, I would hear people say that there were shops, schools, or facilities that a black African man or people were not allowed to enter least of it to enjoy their full rights. Marxism taught us that everything that one had belonged to the state. During my time [in] the training, I never quite understood that one would buy a house and be told that it belonged to the state. But the bottom line, we ended understanding that it emphasized sharing at the individual level and resource management equity. If I have food, I cannot eat while the other one is not eating and starving. We were taught to share and shun greediness. We were taught that resources should be shared equally to benefit every citizen in their area, not to benefit individuals. We never wanted a bourgeoisie system and that is what we were taught. The lessons on Marxism taught that everyone should get all resources and opportunities equally. If our country produced gold then all should benefit in an equal way from the production.

Nkomo taught us that the means of production should be shared equally by everyone in the country and they should give rise to food production and crops. It made us understand that we needed to farm so that the entire nation benefits and does not starve. That's why after the war, ZAPU bought farms to deliver as per our ideology and also to allow members of the party and army to work and manage farms, especially those that … would have failed to gain employment. We had all those things in all our plans but it did not happen in the manner in which we had planned it.

We ended our training at Mkushi in June 1978, and I was then transferred to New Mkushi where I was waiting for further deployment. Before we even did anything at New Mkushi we were bombed. When we got bombed at Mkushi we lost a lot of people. Mkushi was a military camp. We woke up early morning when we were told that Freedom Camp was bombed. All commanders were called for an urgent briefing after the FC incident to be alert.

It was now days without food, for the camp had run out of food. So many female soldiers had to go out in the bush to look for wild fruits like 'umkhuna' and 'amazhanje'[17]. We would go there to gather the wild fruits to eat. Some of us were called for a briefing but I wasn't around as I had gone to look for wild fruits. When I came back, I was told that I was also called for the briefing with other commanders. I ran to where I was called, but when I was almost at the HQ, I found others dismissed and told me to collect my Simonov rifle (SKS)[18] gun like any other soldier who was called at the briefing. My colleagues narrated to me why they had been called, which was to prepare others that anything was now possible now that FC was attacked. We were asked to tell our companies to be alert.

I collected my gun and returned to the camp from the HQ. I wasted no time and I called my company and briefed them of the need to be alert as instructed by senior commanders. Shortly after briefing them, I removed my shirt now that we stayed as girls only.

When I was about to remove the other side of my shirt, I saw black jets that were coming from the Western side of Mkushi and I knew trouble had started. I blew the whistle to alert others to take cover. But while alerting everyone, they dropped bombs and started firing. I ran while carrying my gun, part of the lessons taught us never to leave our guns behind. I ran and took cover as I stood firm in one of the trees straight up and in contact with it. In the military, if an enemy is attacking you in a jet or helicopter you are supposed to take cover in a tree by standing firm close to it. You are not supposed to lay down as the enemy will break all your legs and you won't be able to walk. As I was running away and taking cover, I was exactly doing what we were taught in evading out of an

---

[17]The type of African wild food that was gathered and eaten by female combatants at Mkushi camp in Zambia.

[18]Simonov rifle (or SKS), is a weapon which was widely used in Russia, formerly the USSR. (The Russian 'v' is pronounced like an 'f'.)

obstacle. When they had passed their shooting range, I would move from one tree to the other running to take cover. From around 9 am I was able to walk a period of 200 meters in six hours as it was tough.

Others ran and took cover into thickets of bamboo and grass, so the enemy targeted all those places. They would fire, shoot and drop bombs until the thicket was cleared. They would not stop shooting till the thicket got clear. That's why those that hid inside the thickets never survived. A lot of people died. In some instances, the dropped missiles would charge and lift everything near it like buildings, people and destroy everything. Luckily, Mkushi was sandy and when some missiles fell on swampy sand, it was losing traction and failed to charge because of lack of friction and later failed to detonate. Some ran to take cover near the crocodile-infested river. They dived into the river and crocodiles feasted on them while also the enemy fired. A lot of our people were trying to cross the river and many died. The river turned red and black as dead bodies were floating on top.

Around 3pm, their air force operations of firing and shooting decreased. I'm sure they had gone to reload ammunition and the ground force activities increased. While we were still running we were intercepted by two Rhodesian ground forces wearing brown uniforms, we called them 'Madzakudzaku'[19]. We [thought] maybe they wanted to capture us and they stopped us and surprisingly they were speaking in Ndebele. They showed us which direction to take as an escap. There was no time to hesitate or to doubt when we were afraid. We ran in the direction that they had shown us. We ran not thinking that we would be misled or be trapped. Fortunately, despite hearing gunshits behind us we managed to escape.

We ran and it was almost around 9pm. People were now tired of running and there was no other alternative. While running, we saw a mountain. When we were about to go there, I warned others that I had seen a flame coming from the direction we were headed to. Other guerrillas said I was seeing things that they didn't, maybe I was afraid. I thought maybe it was an optical illusion after a long day. We ended up going under a tree, but I had observed that when we began sitting under the tree, I began to see some trees that I had not seen before we arrived at the place. It was like these trees were becoming concentrated to us when in fact, when we were resting at first, there were none.

Surprisingly, these were enemies that had been following us, using the camouflage tactic of carrying a branch of a tree and standing like it while advancing to us. When I alerted my colleagues who had also seen what I had seen, they shot one among us on her arm. We told her to tie the arm while we were running. We were only able to tie her when we had run a safer distance away from the obstacle.

---

[19]Reference is made to Rhodesian African Rifles.

While we were running away, we met Zambians and we asked them the direction to Rusemfa and they told us that we were almost there. When we got there, she was admitted at Rusemfa and given a drip, I mean the one who was injured. The next morning, we were instructed to go back and pick up the dead bodies for burial in a shallow grave. I faked that I was sick as I was pained by the death of many of my colleagues. I couldn't [accept], as it was a bitter pill to swallow, how they had died. Bodies were then picked and we attended the burial. A lot of the girls had died and we then moved from Mkushi.

What made it worse was the fact that many girls, especially the recruits who had started their training, ran into the pits to take cover and hence the Rhodesians went to the pits to fire and used gun bayonets to kill them while they were in the pits. Those pits became their graves as they were killed inside.

Nkomo attended the mass burial and the Zambian government honoured the fact that the place was to become a monument and up to now it's still a monument. The idea was that ZPRA guerrillas would go there maybe annually to pay their respects but well things did not go well as ZAPU never got the opportunity to govern. Also, the plan was to have the parents/families of the deceased visit the shrine as we had gathered the war dead register. But well, it failed as it is expensive and the Mugabe-led government is not forthcoming in honouring it as a monumental shrine but they developed theirs in Chimoio Camp at Mozambique where they operated. The survivors, can't go there because it is expensive. You young researchers, you are our only hope of capturing such moments. I'm happy that you are pursuing it. All our war dead register was then confiscated by Mugabe-led government to destroy our history.

After the bombing, the party decided to relocate us to Rusemfa and we were further transferred to Kafue at a farm that belonged to Milner,[20] who had offered to accommodate us. After a short while, we were moved to Solwezi which was now a camp. A small group for us were mischievous and wrote a letter to the camp commanders expressing our displeasure regarding some incidences at the camp. We were witnessing unpleasant things and hence we decided to write a letter telling the superiors and exposing the wrong doers. When they received the letter, they were offended and decided to punish me and Sibongile. However, security personnel who were meant to kill us never did. I don't know for what reason but we were only disciplined.

A time came at the camp where all who thought [they] were pregnant had to register their names. I registered mine knowing that I wasn't pregnant. I had to fake a pregnancy to evade the mischief I had done and run away from being killed. I was moved from Solwezi to VC. At VC a doctor had to confirm the pregnancies. He realised that I wasn't pregnant at all. I received counselling

---

[20]He was a Zambian Minister who played an important role liaising with and supporting the liberation movements and especially ZAPU in Zambia. He came from Bulawayo, but had moved to Zambia as a young man in the 1950s and joined UNIP.

before returning to Solwezi. When asked why I had lied, I told them I needed to escape Solwezi because I feared I would be killed. I was assured that no one would be killed and they later changed to a new camp.

I was taken to an N.S.O camp which was Mazowe 2. I stayed at Mazowe 2 for a few months and was later taken for further counterintelligence training in Yugoslavia. I returned home in 1980 from Yugoslavia when other ZPRA guerrillas had returned home. ZAPU was a government in waiting with each department represented. Guerrillas were taken for further training to have qualified personnel in the area. I was taken for further training under N.S.O [I was] ready to prepare a government. I was in the department of security under intelligence and counter intelligence. So that was the training that took me to Yugoslavia. After my training in Yugoslavia, I went to Zambia and came back to Zimbabwe. The state had won independence but we then faced real politics. The victims of colonialism then became killers. It was now a Demobilization Demilitarization and Reintegration. Many of our guerrillas became targeted because ZANU-PF felt intimidated especially [by] those who had intelligence and counterintelligence. My colleagues knew my intelligence status I then dibut I had not disclosed it officially. I was then integrated into the then newly formed Zimbabwe National Army.

Let me end by saying our history has been side-lined deliberately. We were better trained than ZANU-PF, especially our female brigade. Even if today, you give me an AK-47 and Bazooka, I would fail to run because of age but I will surely operate it fully. Our history, it's littered everywhere with photographs. Go everywhere in the country, you will be told by communities of ZPRA, by the people themselves. Things turned out the way they turned to be, most of them not as we envisaged but I can confirm that we ran a good race in all what we did!

CHAPTER 10

'I still do not believe how I survived'

Sevi Dlodlo
(Mkushi trained cadre and survivor of the bombardment)

Fig 25: Freedom Fighter, Sevi Dlodlo, who was trained at Mkushi. She became a military instructor for other female combatants. She is a survivor of the Mkushi bombing. In 1980 she was integrated into the then newly formed Zimbabwe National Army.

My name is Margret Moyo and my war name was Sevi Dlodlo. I joined the war in 1976. What made me join the liberation struggle was the fact that members of my extended family had gone and joined the liberation struggle. I had to follow all my sisters, brother, and siblings.

While other family members had had gone to war, our parents back home used to push us to also join the struggle. For example, Ethel Mutshatshi, one of the pioneers of female combatants had gone to the struggle, and she and others were used as good patriots. Naturally, as time went by, having a family member who joined the war became fashionable so to speak in Gwanda.

Another push factor that made me join the struggle was the radio program by

Jane Ngwenya.[21] She would speak in the radio program inviting recruits to join the struggle. She dramatized her program as if she was watching you. I remember some of her popular words used to be, *'Kanti wena ongafuni ukungena kwabanye uzolwela njalo ukhulule ilizwe lakho uthi umbhobho wakho uzathwalwa ngubani. Wozani lizokhulula ilizwe lenu.'* (You should all come and join the struggle to liberate your country from colonization. Who do you think shall carry your gun when you are hesitating to come? Come and join the war.) Ngwenya spoke as if she was watching you.

Granted that fact, my siblings and other relatives had gone to the war, and the persistent invites from the radio programs, I became more and more determined to join the struggle. But my greatest worry was how did others join the struggle as our parents and the community at large were only saying that people were joining the struggle, but how? You could not wake up or from nowhere decide that today I am going to the war. It was a process, not an event.

As time went by, the colonial regime intensified its oppression back home at Mlambaphele Gwanda. Black people were beaten each day. Livestock was made to be downsized and a lot of taxes that were requested from our parents made the situation worse. I was young but I remember very well our parents were complaining about the regime. During that time, it was now evident that Joshua Nkomo was recruiting people to fight the regime. One day, a sibling brother called Moses came with his friend at home at the crack of midnight. We were forced to wake up and my mother told us, *'Ogwa sebefikile bafuna isikafu'* (guerrillas have come, they need food). My mother had realized that it was Moses her son who had come looking for food, and hence he was now a guerrilla doing a reconnaissance. I did not realize [it was] him, my mother only made it clear when they had left the scene. I then remembered that it was him as I had [heard] the three-speaking using Sesotho language. Indeed, Moses and his friend had come to do a reconnaissance and to recruit more people, especially from Manama.

The next morning, I told my mother that if only she had told me earlier that it was Moses, I was going to join him or at least ask him how one joins the war and more importantly ask him how my other cousins especially Ethel Mutshatshi were surviving in the war. I was reminded by my mother to be patient as my time was coming. In December 1976, guerrillas came via Mapate going to Manama to do a reconnaissance to recruit more school children. At that time, they came and only realized that most of the school children from Manama had gone to school sporting competitions. After that realization, they were forced to recruit anyone that they met along the way. They took school-going children, the elderly, and

---

[21]Ms. Jane Ngwenya was a ZAPU broadcaster based at Lusaka in Zambia. Her program was widely heard inside Zimbabwe and many ZPRA veterans both female and male combatants say they got inspired by her to join the struggle, owing to her broadcasts they heard at home in Zimbabwe. Her full profile and interview have been included in this publication.

women among other things. Anyone who they met was taken along fearing that they might be spied on by the colonial regime. They passed near our homestead and later stopped at the dip tank to recruit more. Many people were following them and running after them. My uncle said, look at what the guerrillas are doing. I then told him that I am also going with them if this was how they recruited others. This is how I joined.

I ran like any other and joined the crowd that was running at the back of the guerrillas. We managed to catch up with the rest of the people at Shashi River. When we reached the river, we crossed. However, one of the local men who was with us returned home. I knew the man as he was working at the local bar. The recruiters feared that the man was going to spy on them together with the colonial officers. We managed to cross in numbers and, for me, I was very excited that the event was a dream come true. In the area that I come from many people came in numbers to join the struggle. When we had crossed the river to the other side of Botswana, we reached a place called Mabulo. In that place, we were instructed to walk a distance while lorries were on their way to ferry us to Gobajango that very day. Lorries intercepted us and took us to Gobajango. We arrived at Gobajango that very night and from then we never saw those that had recruited us from Gwanda. We were introduced to a new group of guerrillas. I'm sure those had returned to recruit the Manama school children who had completed their sporting day.

I got so hungry at Gobajango and felt that I needed a bath. I realized that what I wanted was surely a life full of surprises and with no comfort. At 04.00 am big trucks that were used to transport cattle picked us up. We were all loaded into those vehicles. We were then ferried to Francistown prison where [we] stayed for some time. When we arrived at Francistown, I regretted why I had joined the others who had gone to the struggle. I began to think of my mother and the rest of my family as the type of food and lifestyle had changed. I realized that it could have been better if I remained at home. Other children younger than me were now crying showing regret. I couldn't cry in front of them but the situation was becoming tense by the day. I remember there were also my relatives there in the group that we were with. There was Betty and Tsireretso (both of whom died at Mkushi). They were daughters of my aunt. There was also Tswarelo, Makepesi, Jabulani, and Promise. Other relatives of mine joined us in the later stages. When I say relatives, I mean those from the extended family. One of those I knew from my area who joined with us was Elias who happened to be my husband post-independence.

When we were at Francistown, we stayed a week and a lot of people from my area continued to pour in. That very evening when we had arrived at Francistown more people from Manama who had been pursued by recruiters came in numbers. Francistown overpoured with recruits and hence after a week or so our group was told to move to another place leaving the Manama crew behind.

Our group was taken to Lusaka by a big plane that had a huge freight to carry everyone. We boarded the plane around 02.00 am. We finally reached the airport in Lusaka. At the airport, I saw many cars and lights and thought maybe the lifestyle was now going to change for the better. Alas, three guerrilla crews came about and introduced themselves to us. They began to lecture us about the objective of joining the struggle. They underscored the good and bad of it. They were rough and harsh in the manner in which they explained what we were meant to do and what we were not supposed to do. Maybe it was part of the process and procedures of training, I mean their roughness and harshness. From there, we were instructed to get into lorries to reach another destination.

We moved from the airport to Nampundwe camp. The route was so rough and full of many road bumps. We reached Nampundwe which was in the middle of the forest. Early morning at Nampundwe we were told to wake up, and I heard people reciting war cries and slogans. It was frightening if you heard it the first time. In that morning, while doing morning drills, there was an instructor who was called Thondlwana. He was very rough. They approached us with sticks to beat us up. To them, it was a way to remove the aspect of recruits or civilians. I remember I cried so much. In no time we got assigned a lot of things at once, we were told to jump, run, assemble and sit down. It was terrible and unfavourable I tell you. I was very stubborn; I remember they would beat me up. At times they would make you starve if you were so stubborn. Where we stayed at Nampundwe, there was a farm close by which had a lot of domesticated and wild pigs. Guerrillas would take those pigs, kill and cook, and we were forced to eat those as our relish. I couldn't eat pork. I remember one time I was forced to eat pork and I refused. I was beaten in front of the other recruits.

At Nampundwe, there were no lessons but there were exercises. We would wake up around 05.00 am, go for exercises, and be told to do general housekeeping duties. We would go and take a bath in the nearby dam, some would die in the dam because of inexperience to bath in the muddy dam. We ended up not going there for some time fearing the worst. Changes came when Joshua Nkomo visited the camp and spoke to Kenneth Kaunda to help in improving facilities at the camp. The situation improved a lot when Manama recruits came a week or so [later]. I remember some came still wearing maroon uniforms. At that time, they were few blankets so at times we would sit around the bonfire singing. In that setting, guerrillas would be with the rest of the recruits making you sing and making you do whatever they would be demonstrating. If you failed to comply, you would be punished or get beaten.

Kaunda visited us accompanied by Joshua Nkomo and encouraged us to soldier on and never to deviate. He underscored that there was a need to liberate our nation. Kaunda and Nkomo agreed to relocate us to a new camp which was called Victory Camp together with the new crew that had come from Manama. We left Nampundwe to VC as girls and women and left our male counterparts in Nampundwe. I ought to state that Nampundwe was the first point of call or a college for recruits to see the difficult side of the war. From the Manama crew I remember, Keabetswe Dube (KD) who now stays in the United Kingdom,

Chiratidzo Mabuwa (the then minister who held various portfolios), Blondy, Toyi-Toyi, Florence (Sikhumba), Bhunjwa (from Mapate), Sebenzile Mazinyane (wife to Rtd. Brigadier Abel Mazinyane), and Nompumelelo Moyo whose war name was Gift Tichatonga (wife to Abu-Basutu the current Zimbabwe Ambassador to Japan) and many more I seem to be forgetting. There was another one that I trained with; she was called Ossie Sibanda. She is now a Colonel and Bulawayo District Commander under Zimbabwe National Army.

At VC, life was not so different from what we experienced at Nampundwe. Morning drills, physical fitness, and commissariat lessons were also done there. I have to emphasize that VC was a refugee camp where in-depth military training was not done extensively. It was common that in every ZPRA camp, be it a transit or refugee camp, such morning drills and physical training were the order of the day. I do not remember eating meat at VC. We would eat *isitshwala* (sadza), fish, and other tinned foods. Because of food shortages at times, others would eat wild foods like umkhuna and other things from the wild. Remember, we were so diverse and for us coming to the war did not naturally create new characters. Our lifestyle showcased our background.

Am not sure of the month but in 1978, we were moved to Mkushi. I was among the first group of female combatants to be trained there. The selection had its way. Early morning, we were called for a parade. That morning we were told that some of us were to be selected for military training. For me, they would choose people that they thought would withstand the training. One man who comes to my mind who was present during the selection was Cephas Cele. I remember he appeared as the man of the moment who had the final say regarding selection. I was then selected together with other friends and relatives. I remember Senzeni Mkhonto-Sigoge who was also among our group. When we reached Mkushi, which was a thick forest, instructors were put in companies. We began to construct our toilets, pitch tents and indeed the training had started.

Although, we had male instructors like Castro, Amos, Kumbirai, Theodophilus, and Makanyanga among others. These people were seasoned and at some point, very rough. They did not care whether you were female. I remember Castro, who had come from Somalia, used to say, 'We are here to train ZPRA guerrillas and not females.' It was a statement to illustrate that we cannot lower our military standards from [when] we are training women. That was a big no for him. We would wake up early morning for physical training. Depending on the instructor of the day, some would make you run 8km others would take you up to 10km. Some would faint along the way, and lag. I remember at some point shortly when we began our training, two girls fainted. They later woke up and followed as instructors would tell us of the stories of the lion that if you lag behind chances of one being eaten by a lion were high.

You would run while making war cries and slogans. There was a mix of physical drills and indoctrination. After the run, at times you would do frog jumps, military drills of jumping, crawling, and forward falls among other things. I must say they were also female instructors who had trained at Morogoro and some that had completed training at Mwembeshi. I remember there was Belinda, Phinda, Sithandekile, Jane Ndlovu, and Ingrid among others. We looked up to them. They inspired us in that when we thought we have seen the toughness among the male instructors they were also tougher. What struck me most was seeing Jane doing a forward fall. Forward fall is a drill that requires one to jump from one point in a spin and land with your feet. She was a giant and she did that. It became an inspiration that upon completing our training I also intend to be doing all those skills.

Coming to military lessons, instructors had their subject which they specialised within. Remember, those lessons were delivered in our companies. There were lessons of commissariat which emphasized the objectives of the war, the party's ideology, and self-determination. To me, it was a modern history subject. It taught us not to fight the colonial regime not because they were whites but to fight their system. Topography which involved map reading was taught as well as logistics which is now called the store in the modern discipline.

When we completed our training a selection of female instructors was made among the group. I was chosen to be a military instructor together with others in the group. I remember there was me, Gift Tichatonga (the wife to Abu Basutu), Sebenzile Mazinyane, Rosemary Maphala-Sigoge, Olie Ngwenya (Ossie Mhandu), and Sithabile Sibanda, Keabetswe Dube, and Netsai Ndebele (Mavis) among others. These female instructors who were selected from Mkushi were known as a group of fifty. We were then meant to train recruits. Some who were not selected were deployed in various departments while others went for further deployment.

So recruits came in for training and before they were trying to grasp the military concepts we were bombed. Perhaps before I narrate how that happened, I should state that they had not learned anything to defend themselves nor was there a way in which they could come out from obstacles because they had not learned anything. I remember it was around 10.00 am and we had come from a tea break. Helicopters used to pass through the camp and, in most cases, they belonged to Kaunda's government. Like I said we were coming from the tea break and all of a sudden, a bomb was dropped from the kitchen. As an instructor, I blew my whistle to give a signal to my company to take cover. It was bad. I took cover with other recruits. The unfortunate ones went to hide in the defence pits so what the enemy did was fire bullets in those pits while they were still in the helicopters and later came out of the helicopter to fire in the ground. They then followed pit after pit and killed the defenceless recruits using bayonets. I do not blame the recruits for running to the pits because this is what we were teaching them to do in the case of an emergency. When I think of this I cry.

We ran close to a hundred meters trying to dodge an enemy using the trees. The movement was made difficult as they attacked using helicopters and also, they had unleashed ground force on us. You would spend a good 45 minutes after you had moved 30 meters. Some were shot in front of me, I remember two girls I knew from Manama were shot in front of me. I told those that were with me to head to the Mkushi River which was nearby. We ran to a cave-like stone and went inside it. I then instructed others to squeeze inside it as it was hollow and cave-like which guaranteed more protection. This is how I survived the bombardment. We stayed inside the cave as bullets did not reach out to us but My God, we were seeing everything which was happening. I remember there were some who had hidden in grass and bamboo thickets, the enemy would target and shoot the thicket and leave the land clear.

Also, the enemy was pushing us in the direction of the river strategically. They knew that we would dive into the river. Some ran and dived into the river only to be eaten by crocodiles, and others drowned and died. On the other side, they had treated the land and the river with napalm chemicals, those that came across the chemical got hurt by the chemical. All this happened while I was hiding but also seeing what others were subjected to. It was painful and when I think of it, I cry. I can't say I was clever; it was the Lord that saved me and others. The bombing lasted until midnight. The next morning, we came out and there were many casualties. Some had lost their hands, eyes, legs and had their body parts damaged one way or the other. Some like me who had not developed scars physically had scars internally. I had never seen anthing like that in all my life. Many had died due to blood loss, dehydration, and pain. A bullet is poisonous! We went around to carry the bodies of the deceased for them to be buried in shallow graves. The defence pits later became graves as some died in those pits. Others were going to survive but unfortunately there was a delay in them seeking medical attention. In short, that was Mkushi for you.

We were then moved to Solwezi for some time. I did not do further training but remained there for some time. An instruction was made to use those preparations for us to return home [as we] were on course to mobilize for elections. I was chosen with a group of trained Mkushi cadres, a few male cadres, and some members from the LMG choir to accompany Joshua Nkomo back to Zimbabwe via Harare. We were very happy to have been given that opportunity. Days later we were sent to Bulawayo and given parents to look after us as we were not allowed to go back to our homes. I was given foster parents in Luveve who welcomed me and took me like their own child. While in Luveve, I was responsible for organizing and mobilizing for the party ahead of the elections. We would wake up and begin mobilization and campaigning for the party.

I felt hate looming inside me when we lost elections. I was overwhelmed with anger when the election never came out the way we had anticipated. We knew how we had been cheated but Nkomo had to accept and made us understand how we should embrace defeat. Nkomo was a peacemaker, imagine many forces wanted him to retaliate against the results but he simply accepted. We had to face the reality that we had lost. Days after, buses were organized to take us back to our home and I also had to board mine which was going to Gwanda.

When I arrived there, I saw no one at home. It was locked. I then said maybe they went out. I went in and opened the hut which was a kitchen and slept inside. I had nowhere to go, family members came later after they were afraid to approach me. In some instances others would be rejected by their family members. But for me it was different. I reunited with them. I later went to Sierra Assembly point and was integrated into the then newly formed Zimbabwe National Army. I served there since and retired in 2008. I got married and have children.

CHAPTER 11

'After I had not been chosen to train, I made myself into the camp and trained'

Magret Cheto
(Mkushi trained cadre and survivor of the bombardment)

Fig 26: Freedom Fighter, Magret Cheto who was one of the first group of female combatants to be trained at Mkushi. Upon completing her training, she was selected as a military instructor for the second group. She was later integrated into the then newly formed Zimbabwe National Army.

I was born as Senny Nare in 1961 in a village called Mnyabetsi although some know it as Siboza. Am told I was given the name Senny by the Swedish at Manama Hospital after my mother gave birth to me. I grew up in the area and attended my primary education at Mnyabetsi Primary where I did grades 1 to 5. Back then we refereed to grades as standards. I later proceeded to Hwali Primary to do grades 6 and 7. The school was much further from my home. In the end, I was forced to look for accommodation at a nearby homestead to avoid waking up as early as 04.00 am and walking up long distances. That affected my performance at school. I ended up dropping out as my parents realized that the plan of learning at Hwali was not feasible.

By 1975-1976, I got enrolled at Siboza Primary and proceeded to do grades 6 and

7 respectively. During that time in 1975, my current husband who was residing in my area together with my maternal uncle crossed to Botswana and later Zambia to join the liberation struggle. In 1976, one man came to our house and began telling my grandfather that he knows where Eric (my current husband) and his son (alluding to my uncle) had traveled to and where they are currently staying. He went on to narrate that he had come to check on us.

The guy persisted for days coming at home and knocking at odd hours repeating the same story. My grandfather got annoyed and quickly concluded that he was lying and surely, he was a Selous Scout. The next morning, my grandfather reported the matter to the police officers. Instead of arresting the guy, a police officer came and arrested everyone at home including me as young as I was. We were all taken to Gwanda Police Station. We got detained not in cells but the rooms for almost two weeks. To them, my grandfather was accused of working with ZPRA guerrillas in recruiting local children for the war. They kept on questioning him while we were detained. I was 15 years of age. We were later released after a span. When we got home, stories of people going to the war started to emerge. You would hear closest people or your peers who you hung out with that they have gone. It became fashionable.

One day I then decided that I also want to go and join this thing called the struggle. This was out of a realization that I might be left out when all children in my area had gone. I wouldn't say it was peer pressure but well it was a hype or spirit that forced one to join the liberation struggle. Ironically, I met 4 others who had also developed the same mindset of going to the liberation struggle. This was January 1977. I remember it was me, Sithokozile Mdlongwa (she died at Mkushi), Enoch Mdlongwa, Maritha Nare (maternal aunt), and Amos Ncube.

We travelled and reached Tuli River around 2pm. From a distance the river appeared shallow but as one went in and began to cross it was deeper as other tributary rivers were still pouring into the stream. Remember, this was January and then the rainy season was rainy season. We managed to cross walking in the same direction while holding hands. We got very happy as we crossed over and arrived at a local growth point at Japi stores. While at Japi stores we heard gunshots which caused panic among us and we got displaced. I don't know whether the gunshots were directed at us or not but they managed to displace us and we lost each other. The thing is people were not allowed to move in groups as the colonial regime feared uprisings. I managed to link up later with Amos Ncube but I failed to locate and connect with many others. We walked to a homestead that belonged to the Malimani family to ask for some directions towards Botswana but the family made us stay. We took it as a gesture that they knew better now that they stayed next to the recruitment corridor. Surprisingly, we stayed there for almost a month and a half as Mr. Malimani was also trying to link up with other ZPRA guerrillas. It later dawned to us that he was working in contact with ZPRA guerrillas responsible for recruitment and reconnaissance.

One day, while we were still there, we were requested to climb a tall tree to count the colonial vehicles that were either coming from each direction. This was done so that they note the trends and scenarios so that we cross and a detailed report is given to ZPRA cadres. We did all that for a week and this was our first role in the liberation struggle. I later understood what we were doing when we were introduced to reconnaissance, trends readings, and topography. This was exactly what we were doing. The next day they told us to go as according to them it was safe. Amos was more knowledgeable than me. He was leading the way and we only reached Shashi River around 8pm. When we approached the river, there were a lot of elephants and it was apparent that it was going to be difficult to cross the river. We decided to sleep at the nearby mountain.

Early morning, we managed to cross over and we were so happy that finally, we had achieved the first stage. We began to walk towards the direction that Mr. Malimani had told us but well there were nearby homesteads that were along the river bank. While walking, we saw a tractor and the driver asked us where we were going and we told him that we are going to the liberation struggle to join Joshua Nkomo. He quickly told us to jump into the tractor. We reached a place called Gobajango, found a lot of people who were like us- wanted to go to Zambia. This is where I saw Senzeni Mkhonto (Rosemary Sigoge-Maphala). At Gobajango, a big lorry came and took us to Selibe-Phikwe. At Selibe-Phikwe, we stayed at the prison. We stayed for about a month. A time came when recruits were chosen to go to Zambia but I was left behind because of my surname. I'm Nare, a surname I took from my maternal side and ironically am told most of them originated from Botswana as there is a paramount chief. A lot of people approached me and attempted to discourage me from attending the war saying I should do something noble like pursuing academic studies as my surname was of royal blood. I don't know how they discovered it but the information was moving as we were registering our names at Selibe-Phikwe. I refused and turned them down. [saying] that I wanted to join the liberation struggle. This was the same time when other parents would follow their children and withdraw them. Imagine other recruits had already gone to Zambia and I was convinced to go to school.

Luckily, I ended up going to Victory Camp (VC) which was a refugee camp. Life at VC was very unique. At some point, we got to naturalize the unnatural or normalize the abnormal. You begin to see things that you would have seen earlier as abnormal but now see them as normal. That was the war for you. We slept in a big hanger shelter that was called Big Bhawa. It was big and very accommodating. However, we would be harassed by lice. We ended up normalizing those lice identified with us now that we stayed in the far-removed bush. No wonder, we ended up calling it [lice] Comrade, as it identified with us. During our spare time, recruits would gather and help each other remove lice especially on their hair. It became a hobby for some to help each other in removing lice. There were also bathing sites that only permitted one to be fast in bathing as there were so many people that needed to use the facility. It needed one to time themselves because you would be removed within five minutes.

At VC, I wouldn't say we received military training but indoctrination and familiarization. This was done to remind us of the objective of the war and what we were pursuing. Indoctrination was coupled with physical drills which made us do road runs and fitness exercises. This was done so that in the event of an attack instructors can instruct and people respond and act. Some of the instructors included Cecil who was also the camp commander and there was Madenga who was also called Planet. It was hard, very hard. The thing is I was very young so some of the pain was easily erased by the peer pressure that such a thing was not directed to me alone but to everyone. I remember, at some point at VC, there was a disease outbreak that attacked knees. People would fall and have their bodies shake. I had not seen that the whole of my life. It mainly attacked those that were almost a bit older. Later we got to be told that it was a result of malnutrition. Maybe it was but well, this is what happened.

As time went on, a selection team came at VC to select recruits to receive military training. The recruits were supposed to go ahead to open an all-exclusive women camp at Mkushi. The team was led by Cephas Cele. Cele was a no-nonsense guy and his word was final. When he said you are not going his word was non-negotiable. He [Cele] was going around vetting and when he got to me, he told me that I was not going as I was very young. I moved away and joined the queue in another section. When he reached to me, I was equally told that I wasn't eligible to go for training. He would say, '*Hayi lowu umncane asifuni onana labo popayi ukuthi bayefundela isisotsha. Onana kabasale labanye okijana lapha e-Victory Camp.*' (This one happens to be very young for military training. Young kids will remain with other young kids at Victory Camp). The most painful thing was to see others going and remaining behind.

The next day when lorries came to ferry recruits to Mkushi camp, I went as well together with others. Ironically, when we got to Mkushi, we stayed a day or two and the Camp commander Billy Mzamo called the five of us. He was questioning how we were chosen seeing that we were very young. I remember he asked our age and we all said we were 18 years. It became an issue but after a day or two, the matter was abandoned. Billy Mzamo was later withdrawn from the camp and deployed elsewhere. He was replaced by Moses Phinda and was deputized by Jane Ndlovu who was trained at Morogoro.

The type of training in Mkushi was purely military which was hinged with guerilla formation. We would do road runs, climb gorges, crawl, roll down the cliff and do judo in our various companies. We also learned different types of guns, how to operate, strip and assemble. The training was really hard but as young people, we got encouraged by the fact that we shall train and later be given guns to go and operate as trained soldiers. The training was not for the faint-hearted. We would carry 50kg of mealie meal and sometimes 10kg of sand. I remember if trucks got stuck, we would be required to carry the bags. Imagine at 15 years. At one time my combat trousers got torn and the whole of my bottom back was exposed because of crawling, jumping, and running. I decided to go to one of the instructors called Makanyanga. I approached him and politely asked for trousers. He laughed and made it a joke. He had to say, '*Wena Blondy, kijana, ngiyalithola ngaphi ibhulugwe shuwa*. (Ah Blondy, where will I get a pair of trousers for you). He later gave me one after seeing that I was genuine.

Concerning health matters especially menstrual cycles. Personally, when I was young, I had not come to that stage. But I always ask myself what others used. Perhaps they used small cloths and leaves. I remember twice the occasion they were a consignment that came as aid. It had some long stockings and socks. Many had to cut the long stockings and used them as pants. This is what I remember. It was really painful.

If you hear a ZPRA women combatant saying that they went to an operation, tell them that they are fat liars! It's not clear why the policy was to train us and never to deploy us. Instructors would say we are training ZPRA soldiers, not women. But alas, we were not deployed. Members of the command would tell us that we are trained so that we occupy key responsibilities in the rear while male counterparts were deployed in the front. Maybe if the war had continued, we were possibly going to be deployed in the front. There were male instructors like Kumbirai, Maphani (Titus Magadi), Amos, Ntatshana, and female instructors who had completed their training in Morogoro and Mwembeshi that included Audrey, Constance, Jane, Ingrid, and the other one that I seem to forget but I only remember her because, at some point, she shot one girl in the camp. During the training and post-training phase, I do not remember regretting why I joined the struggle. I was looking forward to training and going to the front as we were earlier promised. I did not regret it. There are instances when during the training I was requested to join others who were chosen to go for a scholarship program but I was not successful. I think on three counts I was chosen but I found myself unsuccessful. I was supposed to be a trained ZPRA soldier.

Discipline was instilled in us and so was the punishment to those that disobeyed orders. Relationships were there at the camps, especially in VC. In Mkushi we would hear this and that among those that had grown up a bit. I remember in our group in Mkushi, there was a lady who was withdrawn from the training after she was found pregnant. She was called Flora Dube. I think she was sent back to VC as that camp was accommodative to such people with pregnancy.

The training came to an end and I was chosen to be one of the 50 instructors to another group of recruits that had come for training. Those who were not chosen as instructors opened a new camp near which was called New Mkushi as they awaited deployment and further training. I was among the group of 50 who was chosen to be instructors. These included Sevi Dlodlo, Gift Tichatonga, Senzeni Mkhonto-Sigoge, Netsai Ndebele, Ossie Ngwenya, Thenjiwe Mkandla, Siphiwe Ndiweni, Jester Nleya, Ntombana, Fina, Abigail Mabetha Gazi, and Ntombiyezizweni Sibanda among others.

The second group of recruits came through and I was among one of their instructors. We trained them but after a short while, we were bombed. It was around 9 am to 10 am when it all started. Others had already eaten and I was with

Tendai Musikwa and Ntombana, who were other instructors. We took our food and we were still contemplating on where to sit and enjoy our meal. We ended up going under a tree that was nearby. As we were about to sit down a bomb was dropped in the kitchen. We ran and lost contact with each other. Whistles were heard from other instructors to alert recruits. From there all hell broke loose. On the eastern side of the camp, the grass was now burning approaching the camp, and on the western side, there was a river. The move was done strategically to crush us and not to evade.

One helicopter jetted and these are the people that spotted Jane Ndlovu and Audrey. They were shot and died instantly. While all this was happening, one of the instructors called Fina who later got married to Kumbirai the male instructor got captured. I do not know whether it was a genuine capture or she had sold out but she was taken into the helicopter and began to call us by names to surrender. She was calling names, Jane, Blondy please surrender. None of us surrendered but she was later released. While I was trying to run, carrying my AK47, the helicopter spotted me and trailed me. Military lessons taught us that when an enemy is using a helicopter it becomes possible for them to shoot when you are on their right-hand side hence one needed to run on the left side.

At all cost, I was running on the left side. I remember at one point they tried to turn around and I also drifted and turned which made it impossible for them to shoot. Luckily, I saw a big tree that had fallen, it was still very green and had a big trunk. I quickly hid in the green leaves and managed to slip very fast under the trunk. They then dropped Napalm and the tree began to burn. They thought maybe I was going to go out and then begin to shoot. They did not realize that I had hidden under the trunk which made it impossible for me to burn and to be shot. This is how I survived. I went back near the camp and only to find a few recruits saying, 'Today's rehearsals were tough.' We used to do rehearsals to sharpen their vigilance and alertness to such scenarios. But they thought that the bombing was rehearsals. I told them to run.

When I realized that they had gone and this was now at night, I decided to come out and run but with caution as I was using trees to hide. I still had my AK47 with one round. I had it in mind that if the worst comes to the worst, I will shoot myself than be captured. That one I was not anticipating for it at all. I decided to take a short break under a tree. In no time I heard sounds, someone coming but going the other side. I was so alert. I wasn't sure whether it was one of us or an enemy. I became brave and said, 'ZAPU', and the other one responded saying, 'ZAPU as well.' She asked who was talking and I said it's Blondy and she responded that she was Siyathemba who was one of the instructors. This name Blondy was not my pseudo name but a nickname which I was given by Dr. Bhutshe who called me Blondy and that name became so popular. Maybe because I was light in complexion! My war name was Magret Cheto. We ran with Siyathemba and we were prepared not to return to the camp as the camp was burning.

We walked and later slept after evading a spotter plane. Midnight we walked and only met a Zambian and asked for a direction. We only managed to reach Rusemfa but at the time we had linked up with others. The situation was very tense and not nice at all. News had reached all media houses in Zambia so I think it was easy for the Zambians to help us. At the assembly point in Rusemfa, we were given food but people couldn't eat because of trauma and others injured. I still suffer from trauma. We were all taken to Kabwe and from Kabwe we were taken to K2 at a farm that belonged to Milner. This was the place where we united, cried together, and shared stories. It was really painful. Nkomo came to K2 and he cried while addressing us. We later moved further to Solwezi. We regrouped and stayed there. At Solwezi the women's brigade was formed. The brigade was formed to take over the responsibility of the ZPRA department at the rear. Getrude was appointed as the brigade commander and Ossie as the deputy. I was now under the reconnaissance department together with one who was called Crescencia.

Nothing much was done at Solwezi, we were now training the regular army warfare by Brigadier General Nic Dube who had trained at Mulungushi and abroad. That's why I still maintain that if the war prolonged further, chances were very high that we could have gone to the front now that regular training was introduced to us. A nearby camp at Solwezi which was a training camp for ZPRA cadres was later bombed. We went there early morning to see, it was painful. Our mission there was to clean up and make shelters. We picked a lot of bombs that had failed to explode because the place was swampy and bombs at times failed to explode because of lack of traction.

One time still at Solwezi, there was a man called Museka who was the chief of artillery. He told us to prepare as we were going for an operation in the front. We got very happy and prepared for drills. While we were busy engulfed by the euphoria of going to the front, Getrude the brigade commander came that very day. She was briefed that we were going for an operation. She, however, responded that she was privy to such and we realized that Museka had lied to us. From that day Gertrude told us never to listen to anyone except her as the commander cleared by the war council. Such a scenario suggests that there was discord somewhere within the rank and file or there were attempts to sabotage and expose one another. A day or two he appeared in the camp and we spotted him [Museka] and we beat him up. Many of us the girls ganged up and beat him up for he had lied to us and perhaps he wanted to sell us to the enemy. He was badly injured. Selections were still underway in Solwezi for further training.

At the end of it all, I was among those that came with a plane with Joshua Nkomo at Harare Airport. We were booked at a hotel although we were withdrawn and made to stay with other ZAPU-ZPRA cadres in Harare at their houses for security reasons. I stayed in Mbare. We were later taken to Bulawayo where I stayed at Mpophoma, Mabutweni, and later at Luveve. We were accommodated by ZPRA cadres as we were now preparing for demobilization and election. We were not allowed to go back home. It was seen as extremely dangerous. We used to travel with Joshua Nkomo in all his campaign manifestos. We were dismissed after the elections when we lost. I went to Sierra assembly point together with other trained women combatants. This was the time when others got integrated into various departments of the army, intelligence, and departments of the state. I was integrated into the Zimbabwe National Army. I am married to a former ZPRA cadre, Section Ncube and I have five children with him.

PICTURES OF VICTORY CAMP

Pictures used in this publication were accessed from the Zenzo Nkobi Collection kept at Mafela Trust and the South African History Archive (SAHA).

Fig 27: (Above): Joshua Nkomo addressing girls and women at Victory Camp

Fig 28: (Right): Trained women combatants hoisting the
ZAPU flag at Victory Camp

Fig 29: (Bottom): Dr. Nkomo took a salute from the ZPRA Commander Nikita Mangena, in presence of the former Zambian President Kenneth Kaunda at VC, which was a facility for women and children. Some of the women were later chosen from this camp to receive military training.

CHAPTER 12

'They saw a Sigoge in me long before I became a combatant'

Senzeni Sigoge Mkhonto
(Mkushi trained cadre and survivor of the bombardment)

Fig 30: Freedom Fighter, Senzeni Sigoge Mkhonto, who was trained at Mkushi. She became an instructor to the second group of recruits at Mkushi who were later bombed. Mkhonto was further appointed as a camp commander at Sierra Assembly Point, which was an exclusive women's camp during the Demobilization, Disarmament, and Reintegration.

My name is Rosemary Mathe. I was born and raised in Manama in Gwanda District at a village called Zelezele. I am born in a family of seven children. We all lived together as a family although there were increased stories of colonial repression. My father would boast of other kids in the area that had gone to join the struggle. In a way, he was encouraging us as well to join the liberation as it became a trend for young kids in the area to join the liberation struggle. More so, there were radio programs that were broadcast, and these programs invited people to join the war to resist the colonial regime. The most popular radio program was that one which was broadcast by Jane Ngwenya. At the time I never used to see the colonial repression that many in the area alluded to but well I ended up having anticipation to join the liberation struggle because of the revolutionary spirit which was now all over. My father did not stop encouraging us in the family to join the liberation struggle. At some point, he said, 'Be like other children in the area that have crossed over to join the liberation struggle.' Indeed, this became a clarion call that our time was up!

In the following days, I liaised with other two cousin brothers of mine to cross over and join the liberation. We became more than determined to go where other children were said to be going. Two days before our scheduled day to cross over to Botswana, we heard that students at Manama High had been recruited and taken by guerrillas to join the liberation struggle. The Manama incident became the biggest motivator to the three of us as we saw no reason of remaining behind if the whole school had been taken. Did we have any reason to remain behind when most of our friends were said to have gone? No! We felt inspired to join others even if we did not know what war exactly entailed.

Our journey began around 2pm when we took off from our homes determined to cross over to Botswana. I must say we did not know the exact way but we had leads that people normally spoke of. We finally reached Shashi and crossed over into Botswana in the middle of the night. The strangest thing I continue to ask myself up to now, is where did I get the courage to walk in the middle of the night? We did not fear anything we were more determined to sail through. After crossing over, our priority was to find where there are people talking and a homestead to ask for directions.

We reached Gobajango after midnight and decided to put up there and sleep. It was not an ideal plan but, well, that was the only option presented by our situation. Early hours of the morning, we saw a lot of people grouping and saying that they were going to join the liberation struggle. This is the time I saw Magret 'Blondy' Cheto who was also going to the liberation struggle and we later met at Victory Camp and Mkushi Camp. While at Gobajango, we jumped into the vehicles that were said were transporting people said to be joining the struggle. Quickly, we jumped in and we were taken to Selibe-Phikwe which was a prison.

At the prison, my cousin's brothers joined other males and I also joined other females. Although some of my peers were regretting why they had crossed over, I did not. I knew that I had the blessings from my father and more importantly, I was at ease knowing that I was not forced to join the liberation struggle but it was out of my will. We did not stay long at Selibe-Phikwe now that there was now an influx of recruits. It became apparent for the authorities to decongest the place. Nothing much was done at Selibe-Phikwe. I think a week or two, I was called with some recruits and we were flown to Lusaka of Zambia. It was my first time boarding an airplane. When we got to Lusaka, lorries came in numbers to ferry us to Victory Camp. The camp was called Victory camp after it was translated from the Portuguese language which was *vitória é certa*. The translation into the English language meant victory is certain. The camp was previously been occupied by the Angolans who later relocated back after attaining their independence. Also, VC was a refugee camp for women and children. The command element also trained male combatants. Cecil was the commander at the camp.

We arrived at VC, we were given the war names that we were supposed to use to hide our identity. The name I was given was Senzeni Mkhonto. I ought to narrate to you that I was later called Sigoge after senior instructors said that I looked tall like the senior ZPRA High Command member, Eddie Mlotshwa-Sigoge. I had not seen him but everyone began to identify me with him using my tall structure. This name Sigoge became so popular that [all but a] few people that I was with during the liberation struggle identified me as Sigoge than Senzeni. At VC, there wasn't much that was done. We were put into companies and did military drills that included exercises, road runs, and lessons of why we had joined the liberation struggle. It was more of indoctrination because the instructors concentrated on making everyone understand why they had joined the liberation struggle than anything. Fine we would do road runs, and exercises but those were intended at removing the civilian character in us and keeping us fit for any eventuality in the camp. To me, I saw physical exercises as a preparatory way for our military training. We had instructors like Makanyanga, Sylvester, and Cecil, who was also the camp commander, among others. There was Grace Mutshatshi, Belinda, Audrey, and many others that had trained in Morogoro and Mwembeshi. They were good in the manner in which they trained us.

The time came when we were called to parade. I think this was in the mid-afternoon. We did likewise and we were told that they needed to choose people that were to be sent for military training. This was a point of difficulty! Nearly everyone wanted to be chosen because everyone was determined to train and have a gun to go back home and shoot as said by Jane Ngwenya through her radio program. As we were standing in a parade, a senior ZPRA officer who was called Cephas Cele began the process to choose and vet. His word was final. We were so many but he would go line by line qualifying and disqualifying others. Luckily, I was one of those that were chosen. What makes me laugh up to today is the fact that he said, '*Wena awusali ngobude bakho lobu.* (Hey you, you will not remain behind. You have been chosen because of your height.) I quickly proceeded and joined the queue of those that were qualified to go to Mkushi to train as cadres in the first group.

Vehicles came by and we proceeded to Mkushi camp. We arrived at Mkushi that very night and we pitched our tents. The next morning real military training began. It was purely military training without any setbacks. We would do road runs, toyi-toyi, bayonet charge, obstacle crossing, judo, and do what was called number 9. I liked the physical type of training for I was very fit [and] executed all my assignments on time.

At Mkushi some female instructors had completed their training at Morogoro who included Jane, Belinda, and Audrey. Some had also completed their training at Mwembeshi like Ingrid Ndlovu who is now Mrs. Nerongo, and I think Dorcas Ndiweni as well. Other male instructors included Ntatshana, KK who was the brother of Vice President Kembo Mohadi, Maphani, Castle, Ishmael, Sotsha,

Mananavira, Kumbirai, Castro, Phinda, and our camp commander Billy Mzamo. The type of training was very difficult although we got used and later enjoyed it more than anything. There were also commissariat lessons, topography, and map reading. All these improved how we thought, executed all our assignments and more importantly cooperated. Discipline was also instilled in us. One would be punished if they disobeyed. One would be beaten, detained, or made to carry out a difficult assignment. This was war! Over and above, we were taught to share and appreciate one another using the name comrade.

We had our pass out although it prolonged as we were told that Joshua Nkomo was held up in other diplomatic processes. I think the training went on and eventually, we completed it. Upon completion, I was among fifty cadres that were chosen to be instructors to the second group of recruits. Some of the military instructors that were chosen in the group of fifty together with me include Gift Tichatonga wife to Abu Basutu, Sevi Dlodlo, Jester Nleya wife to Dubhu Nleya, KD, Abigail Gazi, Ossie Olie Mhandu, Sebenzile Mazinyane, Chiratidzo Mabuwa, Thabisile Shoko (Toyi-Toyi), Sithabile Sibanda and Blondy. There are many others who I seem to be forgetting but were among the group of fifty instructors. Being chosen as an instructor did not mean that all those that were not chosen were not fit. It was never like that. Everyone had a fair share of their role. Others who were not chosen as instructors became the thought power of the struggle while we then became the foot soldiers in training other recruits. All trained personnel were moved from the old Mkushi camp to New Mkushi. By the old camp, I mean the camp that we trained and all trained personnel were ordered to pave way for the recruits who had come for the training. New Mkushi was almost a kilometre or two away from the old camp.

After completing the full military training, we had our pass out. However, it was delayed. As highlighted above, I became one of the instructors to the second group of recruits that had come to pursue their training like us. However, within a short period into the training of the second group of recruits we got bombed. This was in October of 1978. This was a very unfortunate and sad period. If my memory serves me well, an instruction had reached the camp that we needed to be on the alert now that one of the ZPRA camps called Freedom Camp had been bombed. The instruction was that we needed to be alert and take cover as we were likely to be attacked as well. This was intelligence information that had been picked up.

It was in the morning around 10 am when the bombing started. Other companies were still at the kitchen anticipating to receive food. All recruits in my company had already eaten and had already moved away from the kitchen to take cover. Taking cover was in different forms. It meant that everyone occupied strategic exit points that allowed one to be safe, to come out from the obstacle and fight back. When it started, I was out of the red zone which was at the kitchen where they dropped their first bullet. There was a loud bang which I heard. At that moment there was confusion all over as people ran in the direction which they thought was safer for them. When there is a bombardment, you cannot tell where people have fled to, we were all over. What made the situation worse, was the fact that Rhodesians used their air force, rounded up the area, pushed people in the direction where they knew they had already been surrounded. Later, they used their ground force. What we called defence pits later became graves for those that had taken cover there as they were shot inside or at worst killed using bayonet knives. This was terrible!

People died; some fell into the river that was near us as they fled from the enemy. As if not enough, Rhodesians also dropped napalm to make it difficult to escape the obstacle. Some of us fled to the side where there was no water so we were safe. As a company we decided to remain in our positions for some time. Then after a while, we maneuvered, but at that time the Rhodesian ground troops were approaching the camp to comb up. Fortunately, when my company, camewe were moving in a position which was between the units of the ground troops. Some were on the left side, others on the right. They had for unexplained reasons left a space in between and that is how we managed to survive. We survived not because we were clever and more tactical than other comrades but by the grace of God. It was God, but well in the war, we were not taught about God because it was believed that western religion was a progeny of colonialism. We survived as our time to die had not come. We could hear shots fired from the left and right sides.

We hid for hours in that closet. The most painful thing was that you would hear people screaming, crying, and gunshots. This was terrible. The whole day into midnight, we were still hiding. After some time when there were lowered sounds of movement and gunshots, we decided to move. In every military training, some zones or directions are revealed to everyone in the camp to regroup when there is an attack. Our regroup zone was about 30km from the camp at a place called Rusemfa. We decided to move in that direction but we were very alert and vowed not to leave anyone behind. We moved and camp to the main road crossed it over and after a while, we saw a big river once more. We didn't cross over it as we were now tired and very drained by the scenes of the bombardment. We then decided to sleep at that point. Fortunately, where we slept was a stone's throw away from the regrouping zone. We only realized that at dawn when we saw a lot of people regrouped there. We joined others and the mood was gloomy. At that time, I began to look for my other comrades whether they were alive or dead. People were crying, traumatized, and hungry. Remember others were still waiting to be fed in the kitchen.

We were then taken to Kafue at a farm that belonged to Milner. At that time, casualties were receiving treatment and those that had been injured were taken abroad to receive treatment. Joshua Nkomo and other command elements came to Kafue. Surprisingly, Nkomo failed to address us. He cried loudly. Imagine a big man like Nkomo crying! In no time a new camp was opened which was called Solwezi. It was further up close to the Congo-Zambia border post. At Solwezi, we stayed there although we continued with training which wasn't at a large scale as compared to Mkushi. This was the same time when the women's brigade was formed and appointments were made. Getrude Mpala was appointed the brigade commander while Ossie Mhandu became the deputy. We stayed there until the time of the ceasefire when we returned home.

After the ceasefire, we moved to a place called Sierra Assembly Point. Others would call it Sierra camp which is still correct as it was both an assembly point and camp for ZAPU-ZPRA women. I have to mention that it was a camp where women camped there while waiting for appointments from the party, instructions, and later became a coordinative centre for women to be demobilized or attested into the army. Sierra was located in Gweru in the Midlands Province near a place called the Insukamini area. This is why others would call it Insukamini camp as it was close to Insukamini. At Sierra shortly when I came from Zambia, I was appointed the camp commander in charge of the camp. We would receive many women from Zambia and coordinate the activities in the camp. The party had emphasized that I should be the last person to move out from the camp. When others were posted to various departments of the then newly formed army, police or intelligence I became faithful to my superiors and hence I served at the camp. I was the last person to move out from the camp when all activities were completed. I got demobilized from the army and have lived as a civilian since then. I am happily married to Maphala and have four children, that's Wisdom, Lorraine, Naledi, and Molefie.

Fig 31: Picture of the Freedom fighter, Senzeni Sigoge Mkhonto, wearing combat gear at Sierra Assembly point in Gweru. **Picture source**: Accessed from Senzeni's personal archive.

CHAPTER 13

'Our physical appearance and body language also told a story'

Sithabile *KD* Muchachi
(Mkushi trained cadre and survivor of the bombardment)

Fig 32: Freedom Fighter, Sithabile 'KD' Muchachi, who was trained at Mkushi. She became an instructor to the second group of recruits at Mkushi who were later bombed.

My name is Keabetsoe Dube affectionately known as KD. I was born in 1960 at Mnyabetsi village in the Gwanda District. I was recruited to join the liberation struggle in January 1977. Growing up in Mnyabetsi, I had no political awareness or understanding of colonialism but had a vague awareness of the liberation struggle and about Joshua Nkomo. Thinking back, there were often hushed-toned conversations among the family elders about an uncle who had been to Gonakudzingwa and had mysteriously disappeared. Questions about the disappeared uncle were discouraged. The Ian Smith regime Police periodically came to the village to interrogate my father and his cousins about the disappeared uncle. This uncle later visited me in Victory Camp which explained his mysterious disappearance.

Generally, I never saw any anomalies. I enjoyed my childhood, playing with friends, roaming in the local woods, and with the associated carefree village life upbringing.

A time came in January 1977 when the new school term started. I returned to Manama Secondary school where I was already a boarder going to start Form three. Manama was a popular Swedish Lutheran mission school that attracted children from the surrounding areas of Matabeleland North and South, Zvishavane and Mberengwa. Around 6 pm on the first Sunday evening of the new term the school bell rung. The bell ring signalled that we needed to gather at the assembly. From nowhere armed men appeared within the school ground, which was surrounded by a high fence. For some of us fear, terror, and turmoil set in. The men identified themselves as ZPRA and talked about going to "empini".[22] Unusually, the gathered group included teachers, pupils, and other ancillary staff. We were then marched out of the school gate in the direction of the Tuli river which was towards the Botswana border. The younger school children who had started their boarding experience cried and their behavior indicated they were distressed. These young children were all taken to the liberation struggle. We referred to these kids as *okijana*.

I had no idea of what was taking place. I was in a state of shock and confusion. Strangely enough, some pupils were upbeat, especially those that understood the liberation struggle dynamic. In some instances, there was that mob psychology that went like, 'Look my classmates and children from my village are here, hence this is the right place to be in'.

We crossed the Tuli River heading to Botswana. The armed men shouted orders telling us to keep moving in an orderly manner and he demonstrated authority. We walked through the night in what appeared to be a planned route avoiding interception by the Rhodesian army. In the early hours of the morning, there was evidence of Rhodesian army planes flying overhead. On these occasions, the armed men commanded us using the expression 'take cover' until such a time they felt it was safe to carry on. Fear set in with a reality of the possible danger of attack by the Rhodesian forces. The all-night shoeless walk from Manama to Botswana through a thick thorny terrain is still fresh in my memory. I don't remember the first point of entry into Botswana, but I still vaguely recall us being intercepted by large trucks that took us to Francistown where we stayed for about two to three weeks. We slept in dormitories, ate porridge and other unfamiliar foods. This was my first experience in a camp with large groups of people of different ages and different political persuasions. A couple of my classmates were clear they did not subscribe to ZAPU but to ZANU which revealed my inexperience and ignorance of the liberation struggle. However, I felt vulnerable and confused away from my family. All these ideologies which were talked about in the Francistown refugee camp made sense to those who understood the political liberation struggle issues. For me, this was frightening and felt out of control.

---

[22] An indigenous word which means war and, in this case, it means the liberation struggle.

Still, on that, there was a massive outcry from our parents back home who demanded that we be returned to their care as they had not given consent for us to join the guerrilla war. I am not sure of the facts, but we got information that the Ian Smith regime organized for our parents to come over to Francistown to take us back home to Rhodesia. Not all parents were able to come to Botswana. Those of us whose parents came were allowed to see our parents for a limited time in small groups. I recall a sizeable number of classmates who did not return to the large group where we had been gathered awaiting our turn to speak to our parents. Some children returned. When the ZAPU officials realized that some children were deciding to return home with their parents, they quickly spoke to those of us who were yet to see our parents. They thtreatened us and and discouraged us from going back home. They threatened to track down our families and kill us. They also promised that we would be allowed to continue with our education in Zambia. My father came for me but was unsuccessful in persuading me to return home. To this day I can still visualize my distraught father with tears streaming down his face. My father died while I was away at war, and this had a lasting emotional impact on mely. Although it was not an informed decision at the time, I joined the liberation struggle. As time passed, I understood the cause of the liberation struggle.

Shortly afterwards, we were flown from Francistown to Victory Camp (VC) near Lusaka in Zambia. This was my first experience on a plane and naively we were excited thinking we were flying to a better future life. We did not know what destiny lay ahead but that did not stop us from hoping that the liberation struggle would bring a better future.

On arrival at VC, the penny dropped that we were preparing to fight a guerrilla war. Our dreams of an expected better life vanished very quickly. The tough language from the trained combatants gave us an insight into what was to come. VC was a holding and receiving refugee camp with mostly women and children of all ages including babies. The facilities were poor. It was survival of the fittest. The first morning, we all paraded and were given pseudonyms that were non-negotiable. I became Sithabile Muchachi. For some reason, that name was rarely used but my fellow 'comrades', as we began to address each other, they called me KD. An explanation given by other comrades was that there were several combatants named Sithabile and to distinguish us I was referred to KD. I'm not sure how this stuck. All comrades who knew me from the war era whether male and female, called me KD. Comrades who knew me well during the time of the war describe me as an individual who was not shy to express an opinion.

At VC there were a set of compulsory routines, some of which included attending political classes (Marxist doctrine), a regular exercise called "toyi-toyi" and many other chores. I recall the VC camp commander who was called Cecil and other female instructors that had completed their training such as Jane, Audrey, Belinda, Evelyn, Constance, Bvundzai, and others whose names have escaped my memory. These trained female combatants were our role models. Their physique was impressive. They skilfully performed martial arts such as judo and karate. Jane was cool and she commanded authority. One of the prominent male instructors was Sylvester. He was tough and charismatic.

When a new group of recruits was selected to go to Mkushi Camp to start military training, I was among them. We were not privy to the selection criteria used to select recruits from VC. I guess your physical fitness and health were taken into consideration. I remember one of my cousins, who was physically fit, remained at VC because she was pregnant. Sylvester came along to Mkushi as one of our instructors.

We travelled to Mkushi in large open trucks. Our accommodation was tents which were strategically placed. The training started soon after we arrived at Mkushi. We received the full military training which involved daily physical training, foot drills, weapons training, topography, etc. Our initial camp commander was Billy Mzamo, an experienced military instructor. I got the impression that he was not an ordinary talent but an intelligent strategist. He designed a quality training program that fully prepared us for war.

Our training instructors were a mixture of female and male instructors. At times the training involved running in the gorges in very difficult terrain. I enjoyed the physical training more than anything. Some of the combatants I trained with included the likes of Neutral, Sevi, Cecelia, Ossie, Thoko, Daughters, Gift, Toitoi, and many others whose pseudonyms I have forgotten but can remember their real names. Female instructors included Jane, Audrey, Evelyn, and Sithandekile. Makanyanga, a male instructor, I recall as tough and autocratic. Apart from the physical exercises, there were theoretical lessons from a political commissar who ensured we understood the reasoning for the liberation war. The emphasis was that we were fighting for a system where the country's resources would benefit all citizens in the country.

After we completed our training, our pass-out parade was officiated by the Commander in Chief, Joshua Nkomo. Soon afterward I became one of the 50 military instructors tasked to train the next batch of recruits. Most of the trained personnel moved on to a nearby camp and others went abroad to train in other fields.

The recruits arrived but their training was short-lived. Within a week or two Mkushi camp was raided by the Rhodesian army on 19 October 1978 at around 11 am. The first thing I saw from the east were low flying planes dropping bombs followed by paratroopers surrounding the camp. Among the bomb explosions, a whistle was blown too. Tragically, some of the recruits ran to defence pits resulting in them being buried by the bombs.

When the raid started, I was a short distance from the kitchen area, which was within the Mkushi riverbank. From that position, my only escape route was to go towards the river. Unfortunately, the enemy paratroopers had dropped across the river in the direction I was heading. My only option was to take cover in the river. By this time, I had five or six recruits. We hid among the river reeds where there were already dead bodies. Imagine holding your breath in the river amidst corpses and bloody water.

Earlier on, while running, one of my former classmates from Manama lay on the ground severely injured (her legs had been smashed). She called out to me "KD" asking me not to leave her behind. Sadly, due to the nature of her injuries, it was not possible to help her move. This traumatic incident remains fresh in my memory. Her face and name are crystal clear.

The five/six recruits and I were within the river [and] and terrified. Throughout the day we could see the regime soldiers walking and talking along the riverbank shooting where they detected movements. On one occasion late in the day, the regime soldiers walked near our hideout, one of the recruits whimpered. Am not proud of what I did but for our survival and not to be detected I removed my shirt and tied it around her mouth area while encouraging her to calm down. This worked.

We were in the river all day. We escaped in the early hours of the morning, possibly around 3am. We crawled out of the river on our bellies on burnt grass in the dark. The regime soldiers had set ablaze the vegetation around the camp areas at the start of the raid and dropped napalm bombs. We could see small groups of soldiers sitting around fires in the campsite area. We were disoriented. Luckily, I knew the area around the camp and was able to lead the way. We must have crawled for over a kilometre before we were able to stand upright and walk. By daybreak, we found ourselves near the Mkushi camp. This freaked us out. We eventually reoriented and walked away from the camp. We occasionally came across locals who attempted to have a conversation with us but the language barrier was a challenge. Nevertheless, the few locals we met appeared to be aware of what had happened at the camp.

Our physical appearance and body language also told a story. We looked traumatized and dishevelled. I was suspicious of some of the locals. After a long and difficult trek, we eventually regrouped with others at the end of the second day of the bombing at an assembly point. The local radio clearly announced information that helped us. I was disoriented and confused. At the assembly point, we were reunited with other survivors of the bombing. The journey of discovering who was dead or alive, absent or present began. A lot of us were too traumatized to narrate our individual stories of how we escaped.

We were then taken to Solwezi camp. Here a new command structure was formed. Getrude Mpala, who is said to have been trained in Cuba, was appointed to be the women brigade commander and was deputized by Ossie Mhandu. I was seconded to work closely with and stay with Getrude Mpala in Lusaka. From there my sister linked up with me and encouraged me to consider moving to the UK. During this period, there were indications the Lancaster House talks were on the horizon. As others were preparing to return to Rhodesia after the Lancaster House talks, I left for the UK. Afterward, I resumed contact and kept close relationships with some of my fellow 'comrades'.

CHAPTER 14

'I am what I am because of what I got'

Netsai Ndebele
(Mkushi trained cadre and survivor of the bombardment)

Fig 33: Freedom Fighter, Netsai Ndebele, who was one of the first group of female combatants to be trained at Mkushi. Upon completing her training, she was selected as a military instructor for the second group although she was later withdrawn for advanced training in military communication. She was appointed brigade communication officer at Solwezi when the women's brigade was formalized.

My name is Mavis Nyathi, born in Gwanda at a place called Lushokwe. I joined the liberation struggle in 1977 during that time when there was massive recruitment of young people between 13-20 years and during the recruitment of the popular Manama exodus. It was during that time when I joined others from my areas who had been recruited for the liberation struggle. I was not recruited with the Manama crew although we met on our way to Botswana.

Before joining the struggle, I was a student at Matopo High in Matobo district which is run by the Brethren in Christ Church mission. At that time, I began to know about the liberation struggle and Joshua Nkomo. The school had few black teachers and many white teachers that were from Britain and America. There was this lady teacher who was white and always spoke issues to do with the liberation and politics although others criticized her that she was racist and a regime apologist. She would make an inference that black people want independence yet the so-called independent states are hard hit by poverty and suffering. We wouldn't dispute as we knew that she had far [more] exposure than us. When you are young you accept everything. She would use Ethiopia as a case study that when one goes to Addis Ababa, there are more beggars than citizens. The long and the short of it, to her independence was not supposed to happen. To us, her teaching was more racial than factual as she would undermine people and associate adequacy and poverty based on skin colour.

Apart from that, the school also housed those that had tried crossing to Botswana to join the struggle but were later caught, arrested, and sent to Matopo High School to receive education These were school kids who would have wanted to join the struggle. They were sent to the mission as the school was far removed from the border. These were students who had been learning from schools along the borders in Gwanda and Plumtree. These students would come and mingle with us. They would share their stories of the little knowledge and one would feel inspired that well, this is what I want. We would discuss such matters although it was offensive. Back home, I would hear Jane Ngwenya doing her radio broadcast calling us to join the war. Ask anyone, her voice, humour, and the nature in which she packed her program were consistent and next to none! The matter in which she spoke invoked a feeling that if I do not join the liberation struggle, I will be left out all by myself.

A time came when I was at home and I began to see the movement of people running behind people that I later knew were trained ZPRA cadres. Many people went I tell you. While in my village such was happening, a massive one was said to be in Manama mission school where practically the whole school was taken to the liberation struggle. This was in 1977. We went and joined the Manama crew which was identified with maroon uniforms. Imagine, some spent two weeks wearing those uniforms. I was enjoying the moment but reality struck when we began to move away from home. You then begin to ask about where you are going, who will take care of you, and a lot of imagination. War had its questions that it responded to itself without asking. More so, our experiences of joining the struggle are different and so were our destinies. Some began to cry as recruiters began to be strict to follow their instructions the more, we drifted further from home. We crossed over to Botswana and reached Gobajango, proceeded to Bobonong. We were then taken to Selibe-Phikwe where we stayed with prisoners at the camp. What they ate is what we also ate.

We only stayed a few days there and a flight was organized for us to fly to Victory Camp at Zambia. In such huge numbers, we managed to board the plane and travelled to VC. VC was a place where different people with diverse backgrounds stayed there. It was an exclusive place for women only with a composition of the elderly, youths, and young kids. You would find the elderly at the camp, those who were forced to flee from Rhodesia as their husbands had been arrested for political activism and, hence, they feared for their lives. Some families would all join the struggle as the whole family. Exclusively, VC was a women's camp! There were young kids both male and female that we used to call *okijana*. One would wonder how they crossed seeing their vulnerability but these are the people that we had in the liberation struggle. While at VC, I was given a war name that was called Netsai Ndebele but because many from Gwanda and from school that joined the struggle identified me with the name Mavis and hence, I used Netsai and Mavis interchangeably.

With the large population at VC, we would eat *isitshwala*, fish, and beans among other things. The food was as up to scratch as one would expect but well, we were at war not at home. Our sleeping arrangement was such that everyone could be accommodated. Some slept in tents and others in a big room that was more of a warehouse and we used to call it Big Bhawa. In terms of health matters, as girls, we would rely on basic tips that we would do back home.

As the population was increasing by the day at VC as more refugees were still coming in, the authorities decided to select several girls for military training. Of course, we were doing limited military drills at VC like *toyi-toyi*, road runs, and commissariat lessons but that was short-lived. It was never a training base but a transit camp.

One day [in the] morning, a parade was called shortly after a morning meal. We got introduced to a new guy in town who was called Cephas Cele. Cele introduced himself and instructed everyone to queue and a process of selection began. He was very instructive and his word was final. When he said, 'this one no, she is underaged', that was that! According to my analysis, I think for one to be selected you needed to be of average height, not too young, and more importantly, appeared physically fit in the realms of their eyes and assessment. In that vein, I was chosen for military training and we were the first group of girls to be trained at Mkushi. The next day we travelled to Mkushi camp. The camp was along copperbelt road towards Kabwe. Cadres would site training camps from terrains that were off the main roads into hinterlands characterized with a lot of water, and covered with overhead trees with canopies to avoid surveillance. There was a river that was perennially full and there were a lot of gorges that we also used at times to train using them.

When we arrived at Mkushi we began to pitch up tents, ate, and retired to sleep. The next morning, it was training as usual. The training was very hard especially the first days, as they would strive by all means to remove the aspect of one being a civilian. It was strictly combat training which was inclined to guerrilla type of tactics as opposed to conventional. We were introduced to war tactics, how to handle the gun, land mines, first aid lessons, and moving in the terrain. At some point, we got taught how to handle explosives and how to react when faced with them.

There was also physical training which included fitness, road runs, judo, close-quarter fighting, bayonet fighting, and gun teaching lessons. In the training, we got taught defensive mechanisms and the manner of response in the crisis period. Commissariat lessons were also taught. The lessons were all about Marxism and

Leninism. It was all about teaching us the norms and objectives of the struggle. War had various key subjects which are now branded differently in the modern-day. I remember there were days where we would be made to carry 50kgs of mealie meal when delivery trucks got stuck along the way to deliver. We would intercept them and come back with the mealie meal. What I loved the most was the concept of fairness in the training. There were no sacred cows. The treatment was the same. If an order to run 5km was made, we all ran that whether your relative was an instructor or not. On that note, there was an issue of punishment when one did wrong. Punishment differed depending on the gravity of the matter. Some would be beaten, given extra assignments, or subjected to hard drills. This was done to set an example for others.

Initially, there was a company of Zambians that came to provide military training but eventually [they] left and new instructors came on board. At Mkushi, there were ZPRA instructors that had trained in Morogoro, Somalia, and the Soviet Union among other nations. The camp commander was Billy Mzamo but was later replaced by Moses Phinda in that position. Other instructors included Kumbirai, Sotsha, KK (brother to Kembo Mohadi), Maphani, Witness Tshuma, Morgan Chindiya, Ntatshana, and trained female combatants that had come from Morogoro and Mwembeshi. These were Grace Muchachi, Jane Ndlovu, Sithandekile Dorcas Ndiweni, and Ingrid. We saw them as our role models.

After the training, I was chosen among the group of fifty that were chosen to be military instructors for the second group. However, shortly before Mkushi was bombed I was withdrawn and selected for further training in military communications in Yugoslavia. I joined them later at Solwezi when a brigade was formed and only to be appointed as the brigade communications officer. The women brigade was formed at Solwezi.

Post-independence I was integrated into Zimbabwe National Army under the signal department. This was because of the training that I received during the liberation struggle. I then advanced my knowledge at Bulawayo Polytechnic studying as a telecommunication technician and later did a degree in telecommunication. I retired from the army and now have ventured into businesses. It is the skills I acquired from the war that has shaped my entire life. I'm married and I am Mrs. Gonde.

CHAPTER 15

'I was happy that before the independent nation, there was Nation!'

Jester Chivi
(Mkushi trained cadre and survivor of the bombardment)

Fig 34: Freedom Fighter, Jester Chivi, who was trained at Mkushi. She became an instructor to the second group of recruits at Mkushi that was later bombed. Post-1980, she joined the civil service and became a teacher.

My birth name is Jennifer Nkomo. My war name was Jester Chivi. I was born in 1960 at Gwambe village in Plumtree under Kandana headman. I am born out of a family of five children, that's two boys and three girls. I did my primary education at Gwambe school and proceeded to do secondary level at Minda Mission in Maphisa, Kezi. Minda mission was a Roman Catholic School. During our time the school had white teachers and few black teachers.

While at Minda it is then that I was politically conscientized of the colonial oppression as there was a certain man at school who would come at weekends to teach us about black and white oppression. He would state how whites were oppressing us the blacks. I should think he was also a teacher or an ancillary staff member at school. From all his engagements, one then began to see how the situation was like, especially of oppression by the whites. The man was a gifted orator who would end his talk by requesting us to join the liberation struggle by any means necessary.

In 1977, schools closed and I boarded a bus from Maphisa which was going to Plumtree via the Bulawayo route. Along the way shortly after the bus had travelled 20km away from Maphisa, ZPRA soldiers intercepted and stopped the bus. They were carrying guns and later jumped onto the bus. I expected the worst from them but well they were very calm and spoke gently. They invited all those that wanted to join the liberation struggle to join right away. A few came out of the bus and followed them up. Then, I had not made any decision as to join the struggle or not. They jumped out of the bus together with others that had said they wanted to join the struggle. We proceeded with our journey and arrived home.

While I had arrived at home in Plumtree, I began to ponder what that man at school used to tell us and what had happened to us on the bus as we were traveling. This troubled me. I began to realize the type of oppression that blacks were subjected to but then I was very young then. During the holidays, I used to help out at Nleya shops as a shopkeeper. I used to do this every holiday. This time at that shop, there was a guy who I considered as my brother who was always lecturing me and others about the liberation struggle and how we as blacks were oppressed. It came to me as a surprise as many people since school had been talking about this matter. You could see in the manner in which he spoke that he was now emotional. He was telling me that look you are assisting her but you will be paid peanuts from it. This guy ended up convincing us, that's others I was working with, to join the liberation struggle and leave all this. A guy called Khahlo and I convinced each other to join the liberation struggle.

The next morning, we went to Khahlo's place to her young sister who was called Beauty and our journey began. We walked heading to the border post, passed Mphoengs and we arrived at Ramokwebana border post. We did not end there; we crossed the border but shortly when we were about to leave the vicinity of the border we got arrested. They threatened to beat us up but they did not. However, they interrogated us, where we were coming from and going. We told them that we had run away from our homesteads fearing persecution by the Rhodesian government and hence we wanted to the liberation struggle. These officers laughed at us and they told us to sleep there and wait for an instruction.

The next morning, they took us to Francistown where we met a lot of people that wanted to join the liberation struggle. Some were coming from Gwanda, Beitbridge, Zvishavane, and Mberengwa among other areas. This was the last time I saw Khahlo as he was told to join other boys as Beauty and I joined other girls at the camp. We couldn't request to see Khahlo as it was not allowed to visit each other or be seen together. The Manama group of girls and boys had not yet arrived then in the camp. We stayed there for a week. Life was quite normal there as nothing was done. We would eat and do a few exercises although the space was too small, it did not permit us to carry out such. We slept in the prison,

94

imagine you had your bed there and a pit which was used as a toilet. This was terrible! Such experiences are still a wound to me. The type of food we ate was also not the best. We ate oats a lot but you would see a lot of flies and other bugs in the oats but, well, we ate. There wasn't an option.

In no time we were taken to Victory Camp and arrived there. We got vetted and we were now under the camp commander who was called Makanyanga. This time we were now many as the Manama crew had also come into the camp. Life at VC was life. We used to do military drills which were more of an indoctrination exercise. It was not a training camp but a refugee camp where everyone was taken on board. Imagine we had the elderly, young kids that we called okijana and the youths. Some families had joined the struggle and left no one behind, and people with those kinds of situations were all taken to the refugee's camp which was VC. I was among the group of girls that were selected to pursue military training at Mkushi. The selection process was based on various factors that they looked at. Your height, age, physical fitness, and asked your level of education. They needed to strike that balance.

I was also selected as one of the girls to train at Mkushi in the first group. At Mkushi, Billy Mzamo was the camp commander and was assisted by other instructors like Moto, Kumbirai, Phinda, and Ntatshana among others. The training was tough and very tough. We used to wake up around 4 am and do road runs. Most of the time it would be cold as the camp was surrounded by the river and swamps. It was very tough and I found it difficult. After the road run, we would return for our breakfast. Food was there but the time for one to eat was curtailed. It was tough. The most unfortunate thing was the fact that we had not developed coping mechanisms to eat, as we did during our last days as trainees. For example, we devised a way that when you would be served with hot oats, we poured cold water in it and drank it. It was better than not to eat at all as we were given limited time. The taste of the food never mattered at all.

One more thing which was also a challenge was the size of combat uniforms and shoes. We ended up wearing them like that as there wasn't any other option. We ended up swapping combat regalia because of the sizes. The combat boots, had no sizes that would fit us. What we ended up doing was to tear our blankets and put some stuff in the boot to make it fit. It became a challenge when you were training as instructors like Kumbirai wanted people to run, never stop, or find a reason to stop, whatever they wanted from you to do. The guy was tough and rough. If you decided to do something fun you would be beaten. I remember one time during the road run exercises, I used to run with this friend of mine who was called Cecelia. We would run with others and swiftly hide at a point where we would join the group when they were running back to the camp. We did this to avoid running. We did this thrice. We were playing truant. On the fourth time, I think someone reported us. Phinda beat us. The guy had to bash us as if we were caught selling out information to the enemy. We were made to dig a trench as punishment. I will never forget that day!

Six months later, upon completing the training we delayed having a pass-out parade for unknown reasons. Others opined that Joshua Nkomo who was to officiate was held up in other processes. What I remember is after the training a group of senior military personnel came to Mkushi to assess while we were still awaiting a pass out. I don't know whether they were assessing the nature of our training or what. I remember in one of the parades when they were still there at Mkushi, Ambrose Mutinhiri and Tshile Dubhu Nleya all agreed that we needed to do another month of training. They said this while in their jovial moods and laughed at us. Finally, the pass-out parade came and a selection of a group of instructors was chosen.

This group of instructors is famously known as a group of fifty. I don't know what criteria they were using to choose but I still believe that physical fitness, age, height, and the level of educational background all contributed to being chosen. In our group some people were very fit and couldn't be left out. People like Sevi, Ossie, Senzeni-Sigoge, and KD. These were fit I tell you. I think I was chosen in the group of instructors because of the level of my education because in the group of fifty when it came to some issues that needed writing and administration I was called to help together with Cecelia, Neutral, and Martha Mathonsi.

As an instructor, I worked with Sevi in the battalion that we instructed. Like I said I mainly focused on the theory side of instructing and Sevi and others took the practical side like road runs and judo. Sevi was very fit I want to be honest. Still on that, within the group of fifty instructors' departments were formed to fully operationalize the training. There was an administrative unit, artillery, reconnaissance, security, and training. I was then assigned to be the chief of artillery specializing in anti-air and Sevi was my deputy. Therefore, our battalion was responsible for the security of the camp. This was a military structure that was put up to operationalize the training. A lot has been said by others that the women brigade was formed at Mkushi long before Solwezi. I wouldn't be absolute to say the brigade was formed at Mkushi and formalized at Solwezi. What is clear to me is that an operational structure to facilitate the training of women was set up at Mkushi and operated within the command of the camp commander who was Moses Phinda and not as a separate structure like what formed at Solwezi.

The previous day to the bombardment of Mkushi, there was a disagreement between Phinda and Jane over something that was not clear. Remember, Jane had assumed a position that was more of a deputy camp commander although I think it was not in black and white. Even if it was, I think the likes of Moses Phinda and other male characters had not fully accepted the fate of women in the command structures within a training camp. It is normal in any society! To be challenged in decision-making by someone you consider your junior makes it feel worse, but look Jane had trained with men that were now seasoned guerrillas in the front. Back to that story, there were disagreements over the withdrawal of sentries from guarding. We were then called for a briefing that requested instructors to be on high alert and be vigilant. As I was responsible for the artillery, we were instructed to withdraw anti-air machinery and other machinery. We complied and security personnel was also warned to be on high alert as Freedom Camp was bombed. One of the security personnel that I worked with was Moses-Mzila Ndlovu. He was at Mkushi sometime but I don't know whether he was there during the bombing. Ndlovu had specialized in anti-air, strella, light machine gun, and security.

At Mkushi we had dug trenches which we used to accommodate recruits on days when they had no drills depending on their company. We would go inside the trenches, cover ourselves with leaves and relax. Covering themselves with leaves meant that the enemy won't easily recognize the recruits. We wouldn't leave the tents pitched when there was no one inside. The rule was to pull it down and only pitch it up when using it. On the day when we were bombed, it was around tea break time between 10 to 11am when companies were feeding at the feeding site in the kitchen. My company was still awaiting its turn to be fed. As my company was waiting to be fed, I decided to go to my tent and sleep for a while. When you finally become an instructor or assume a position of power you end up bending rules and doing what you want. I had to go and sleep for a while.

I never saw anything as I was sleeping in the tent, I heard a loud sound which was a bang and producing vibrations more like a tremor. I quickly moved out of the tent and what I saw was very bad. You couldn't scream, cry or wait to make sense of it but only to run in a panic mode. I ran in the direction of Mkushi River and two colleagues of mine were following me. I realized it was Beauty that I had joined the struggle with as she was always with me. I could not clearly see dead bodies because the place got misty due to bombs and bullets from the Rhodesian air force and ground force. Fortunately, we ended up taking a route that led us off Mkushi River.

As we were running it became so misty and we ended up crawling. These were all the tactics we were taught to use. We reached a certain place that was safer. It was not because we were clever or what but I do know what led us to that place. Many people were pushed to the river and swamps and most of them never survived because they were ambushed and persistent use [was made of] napalm. In our camp, they pushed us into the swamps, and in the other camps, they were pushing them into the river which was infested with crocodiles. This was their strategy that one survives the attack as they fought using the air force, ground force and further used napalm to burn everything. What I remember, is when we got to that safer tree still with Beauty and three others, I had lost my shirt. I was now naked and had only the trousers. I don't know whether I lost it or removed it because of confusion, I don't know. We slept under that tree as the bombardment continued hours into midnight. Others got lucky that they ran in the direction of Rusemfa which was an assembly point in case of emergency. We were completely lost and stayed in there for 3 days. Imagine you are stuck for 3 days without food or shelter.

We only got rescued by Jewel, Stanley Gagisa Nleya, and Tshile Dubhu Nleya, who were doing rounds of assessments. It is a common occurrence for members of the command to do rounds of assessments within a bombed area. You won't believe this, but this was the first time Tshile Dubhu Nleya saw me and spoke with me amid the crisis. Imagine, this is the man who later became my husband. I won't hide this, and will never be ashamed to say that when he saw that I was naked without a shirt, Dubhu removed his and gave it to me. The three of us got closer to Dubhu as we were scared and we were prepared to follow them wherever they were going. They pitched a tent next to us, gave us glucose, water, and later food for us to eat. They left behind Jewel with us to protect us and their trail while Dubhu and Stanley proceeded to the camp as they were on a mission to assess.

On the fourth day, a land rover came which was taking anyone who was still in the bush, took us to the police station. I think it was doing rounds of picking up everyone stranded and injured among other things. They took us to the police station and later to the hospital. At the hospital they assessed me and I was considered healthy. I think before we went to Solwezi, we were accommodated for a while at one farm which belonged to Milner. We then went to Solwezi and this is where the women's brigade was formed incorporating trained personnel from Mkushi. The brigade was now a predominant structure of women as opposed to the structure we had at Mkushi which had also men.

At Solwezi, this is the time I saw Dubhu and developed a relationship. I was later posted to Lusaka where I became more of an administrator within the close security of Joshua Nkomo. From Lusaka, I went to Victory Camp as I was now pregnant. Others were also pregnant at VC who had been withdrawn in various departments so that they concentrate more on pregnancy than work. It was already the time of ceasefire and others were now preparing to return home. As others were traveling back home, I remained behind as I was due to give birth. Now I did not know what to do as Dubhu was nowhere to be seen and at that time he had been promoted to deputize Lookout Masuku. I was prepared for anything, to say the least.

A guy called Nkomeni Nleya who was the uncle to Dubhu and was working at Zimbabwe House came to rescue me at VC. He did not say anything to me but took me to his house. At that time, he did not disclose anything to me that he was the uncle to Dubhu or related to Stanley Gagisa Nleya. On the 10th of April 1980, I then gave birth to a son at Lusaka UDH. I was eager to see my parents but I was afraid of going home as I went to war without a kid and only to return home with one and worse still, I did not know where the father of the child had gone to. This was a struggle (she laughs). I flew back to Zimbabwe and landed at Joshua Nkomo airport and this is the time I saw Dubhu who was accompanied by some of his colleagues. Fortunately, Dubhu had arranged with my brother called Nicholas Nkomo for negotiations and lobola arrangements. I got married to Dubhu and named our first son, Nation Nleya in honour of our struggles that bore the nation!

98

I did not go to the assembly points given my standpoint that I was now a mother. Of course, I went through the process of being attested to the army but Lookout Masuku advised me to go back to school as I was 20 years old. He advised me well now that he knew that I had a relationship with Dubhu. I then went ahead and enrolled at Species college where I did my ordinary and advanced level. I later went on to do the secretarial course only to complete it and enrol at United College of Education to train as a teacher. I have taught at Mtshede, Maphisa, and Greenfield Primary. I have taught at Greenfield for 21 years. I have four kids Nation, Success, Linkman Prosper, and Buhlebenkosi. We have eight grandchildren.

CHAPTER 16

'I was not forced, I joined voluntarily'

Irene Moteletso
(Mkushi trained cadre and survivor of the bombardment)

Fig 35: Freedom Fighter, Irene Moteletso, who was trained at Mkushi. She is among the survivors of the Mkushi bombardment. In 1980 she was integrated into the then newly formed Zimbabwe National Army.

My name is Sehlule Ngwenya. I became Irene Moteletso during the liberation struggle. I was born in 1960 in the Mapholisa area at Plumtree. I am the fourth born in a family of ten children. I did my primary education at Embakwe mission from 1968 to 1974. I couldn't proceed further with my education as it was now a challenge for my father to pay for my school fees now that our family was very big and more importantly, we were all dependent on his meagre salary. I was forced to work at Embakwe mission for almost five months. I worked from January to May 1977.

There was a friend of mine who was called Jane Tshuma who I grew up with. We decided to join the liberation struggle after a series of factors. First, the greatest recruiter was the broadcast from Jane Ngwenya. Her message resonated with my plight and I ended telling myself that if I join the war, perhaps I will be able to fight and be able to go back to school and learn.

Second, in my area where I hail from, there was a prominent businessman called Scotch Ngwenya who was allegedly accused of selling out information to Rhodesians especially individuals or households that supported ZAPU. Community members were forever accusing him that he would sell out information whenever there was the presence of guerrillas or private meetings in the area. Resultantly, Rhodesians would take his word and burn houses and at worst kill anyone who would have been reported by Ngwenya. It became difficult as my parents were staunch ZAPU activists and they were always harassed by the Rhodesians and their apologists like Ngwenya. As a retaliation, ZPRA guerrillas took his son to Zambia and forced him to be a guerrilla. His bottle store got destroyed by guerrillas in front of everyone. Upon destroying his bottle store he was killed in front of the community members as an example to deal with the sell-outs. His body was left unattended for nearly 2hours. I saw all that although I was very young. This was scary!

In May 1977, I decided to join the liberation struggle fearing that we would be killed at home as my family was targeted. They knew that my family supported ZAPU and would hold meetings. Coupled with that, my uncle was always in and out of the police station for supporting ZAPU. This was why I felt determined to join the struggle to carry the gun as instructed by Jane to deal with all the painful episodes that I was going through. I left home with one girl who was called Jane Tshuma as we felt that we needed to go and join the liberation struggle to solve some problems back home.

We crossed to Botswana and we arrived at the nearest police station at Tsamaya for we had had stories that information of anyone who so wished to join the war was found at police stations. At the police, they asked us where we were going and we made it clear that we wanted to join the liberation struggle and fight the colonial system. In response, they asked us where we had come from and from which area. I should say that Botswana people were so cooperative when one sought more information. As a nation, we owe a lot to them. The police officers then requested us to wait for the lorries that were ferrying anyone who intended to join the struggle. Lorries came and took us to Francistown and we met a lot of Zimbabweans who were anticipating joining the struggle.

In Francistown they did not receive anyone, there was a vetting exercise that was done at the camp by ZAPU. You would be interrogated as to why you decided to join the liberation struggle. Some of the questions that were asked requested one's name, their village, and the reasons why one decided to join the struggle. The reasoning behind vetting was prompted by the fact that there was widespread infiltration and the fact that others were fugitives who were evading their criminal offenses using the liberation struggle. I was also interrogated together with my friend and because we understood the objectives and context of the war, we were able to tell them that we wanted to join the war to liberate our country.

Others at Francistown were withdrawn from the camps by their parents. We stayed at Francistown for a while which was about two weeks. At a personal level, I was anticipating seeing what the struggle entails and was not nostalgic about going back home. All I wanted was to train and be given my gun as instructed by Jane Ngwenya, to shoot and liberate Zimbabwe. There was another group that we were told were ZANLA recruits who were also waiting to go to Mozambique. We would wake up and be given commissariat lessons on the objective of the struggle. Of course, we would do military drills but that was not so rampant because the space did not allow such kinds of activities. We would sing and the emphasis was that we must tolerate, appreciate and love one another to fight the colonial regime.

After two weeks, a plane came over and took us to Zambia. On that plane, there were only 45 people and one of the people in my crew was Molly Mpofu, one of the famous people among the veterans. Two lorries came to the airport to pick us up. This is where I saw soldiers that were wearing what we used to call rice combat that came from Russia. Remember, by then I was a civilian, so this guerrilla that came by was very harsh and very authoritative. It was my first time to see and hear how they instructed us to jump into the lorries.

It is then that I saw that what I was anticipating to do had come by. We travelled and reached our destination at Victory Camp. VC was a refugee camp that accommodated women only with the elderly, youths, and even kids. Given the huge number at the camp, some would snatch each other's blankets because blankets were a scarce commodity. Newcomers at the camp often had their blankets snatched away from them at night and their shoes stolen. I experienced that. At VC we used to eat well - beans, sadza, and breakfast among other things. We used to learn things of personal hygiene, objectives of the war, and above all to love each other and appreciate one another in our diversity. We persistently called each other comrade which was a term that cultivated oneness and togetherness although we also called lice as a comrade. Lice were a common feature in the camp as they gave hard time in the camp. We ended up calling it comrade as it was a common feature to us at the camp. We stayed at a place called Big Bhawa although when the camp grew too large ..., we ended up pitching tents as per your company and platoon.

Training at VC was not very rampant. We did mini-training. I wouldn't see that as training but indoctrination that was meant for us to appreciate that we were pursuing war and not pleasure and leisure. We would wake up in the morning and go for a road run, and other drills. At VC some instructors included Audrey, Jane, Sylvester, Cecil, and many others. A time came when we were told that they needed some recruits from VC for training at Mkushi. I was chosen as one of the recruits to receive the training. Others ... were left behind at VC. We travelled to Mkushi and arrived very late.

At Mkushi we were put into companies and there were eight companies. The first four companies were the first battalion and the second four happened to be the second battalion. This was done to manage the affairs of the camp. We pitched tents and we stayed there for quite a while. There was Phinda, Amos, Makanyanga, Billy Mzamo, Mighty Ntatshana, Sotsha, Ingrid, Moto.

The training was tough. I remember there was an instructor who was called Moto, he would blow the whistle so loud around quarter to 4 am. His first whistle was meant for one to wake up and the second whistle was meant for one to run to the parade square. At parade square, they would take a roll call where they counted people present and identify those who would be missing, sick among other things. After the roll call, we proceeded to do toyi-toyi which was a road run that enabled one to run while chanting slogans and singing. Upon completing the road run we would do military drills that made one jump, crawl, roll depending on what the instructor wanted us to do that day.

Breakfast was usually served after physical training. There was not ample time for eating. How we were instructed to eat was systematic in that you eat while standing and you would be timed. Imagine eating hot porridge. We got used to it. We also had lessons that included politics, commissariat, tactics, topography. All these were taught under a tree by instructors. At times after lunch, we would go for route march where we would walk 20km to test our endurance. During those route marches, we would do battle drills of what needs to be done when you are losing the battle, winning, or withdrawing. We would also do bayonet charge tactics, handling the guns and fighting the enemy using the gun at different levels. We would be taught what to do in terms of an attack. We would also do rehearsals of what to do in case of an attack and we would be required to skirmish. Instructors would use live bullets so as get used to the sound and the scenario. Unfortunately, one time when such a rehearsal was carried out three recruits died on the spot. This emanated from the fact that one instructor mistakenly shot those recruits. This was sad. One of them was related to me, and the other two were from Tsholotsho and Gwanda respectively.

At Mkushi we used to have challenges of food supply. We would go for days without anything to eat. At times lorries meant to deliver food supply at the camp would get stuck in the mud. We would intercept them to carry the food to the camp. We would carry 50kgs of foodstuffs. The main challenge to the short supply of food at Mkushi was because Mkushi was a training camp and countries were not willing to extend food aid. Those that supported us only gave us military artillery supplies and no food. It was a different case to VC which had an abundant food supply as it was a refugee camp. During training, I remember we lost one girl who was from Mberengwa after she ate a poisonous plant because of hunger. It was very unfortunate. Drought in the camp drove them to end up eating anything. It's true, we ended up experimenting on anything but well they were unfortunate she died.

We did our pass out although it was delayed. During the pass out Joshua Nkomo emphasized that the army had allowed us, women, to train so that we occupy different departments in the rear and not to be deployed in the front. According to his words, Nkomo made it clear that the strategy was to have trained women taking charge of every department at the rear as we were a government in waiting. Possibly, if the war had prolonged perhaps, we were going to be deployed in the front. I was not chosen in the group of fifty instructors and the trained personnel were requested to open New Mkushi which was nearby to pave the way for the second group of recruits. New Mkushi was 2km away from the main camp and mainly for trained personnel. We continued with the type of training, the road runs, and doing rehearsals of what to do in case we are attacked, although we had reduced the level of the training. Others from our camp had been deployed elsewhere for further training and scholarships.

On the 19th of October, the day at which we were bombed, the then camp commander of the New Mkushi who was Moto called everyone for the parade and informed us that Freedom Camp had been bombed and as such, we needed to be on high alert. He stressed to us that it was unknown which was the next camp that would be targeted. He reminded us to adhere to the protocols of where to gather if the situation got out of hand. Unfortunately, at our camp, we had gone for days without food and we only relied on powdered milk which we had to drink now and again because there was no food.

On the day when our company was now on its way to going to the kitchen to drink milk, a bomb was dropped. What they did was that they were shooting our camp simultaneously with the old one. Their strategy meant that those at New Mushi who were close to the river were pushed to the direction where they would run to the river and be ambushed there. While those at the old Mkushi were pushed to the swamps and got ambushed there. I ran with others and hid in the thicket, although others did not survive as they would drop bombs and napalm which made it hard for many to withstand. I still do not know how I survived. We stayed there for hours hiding. After protracted hours of bombing, they sent the ground force down to take over the operation. Where we were hiding, they passed the area at a distance of 2 meters. Imagine if they had seen us! But we survived. The night before the bombing I had a dream about my father instructing me to be brave and use a way that he was showing me. I took it lightly but it made sense when I pondered deeply while I was hiding. We managed to come out of the thicket and passed by the kitchen and the Rhodesian forces were at the kitchen singing.

We bypassed them and used the other route, othercomrades used a different route. I do not know what happened but within seconds we heard gun sounds coming from their route. Possibly, they were killed. I proceeded with three comrades and walked up to the point when we decided to sleep. We slept there. Where we were sleeping, we got frightened by two lions that were moving in the opposite direction. Those lions stared at us, and we didn't want to move an inch fearing the worst. They stared at us and the other one turned its back and left which made the other to follow suit. This is how we survived.

We managed to run in the direction of Rusemfa and finally arrived there. We met other comrades and we were given food there. On the same day, we were ferried to a farm that belonged to Milner where we stayed for some time while others were treated and attended to by health officials. This is when Joshua Nkomo came through and addressed us. He was emotional and cried. In his address to us he said,

> *'Bantwabami ngilusizi kakhulu kulokhu okuliveleleyo. Sizaqalisela ngaphi? Ngizafika ngithini ebazalini benu? Mhlawumbe ngabe belihleli duzane laba newenu aluba balisizile lathola ukuphepha. Kodwa kungasenani asibambaneni silwe lesitha'* (My children, my heart is heavy, bleeding, and very emotional because of what happened. What will I say and how will I account to your parents? Perhaps, maybe if we had known we would have set up a male camp next to your camps. Maybe the level of damage would have been manageable. However, let's continue to work hard to fight the colonial regime).

We stayed there for some time and later moved to Solwezi. When we moved to Solwezi I was chosen to do a police and security course. I did that course at Solwezi and this was the time when the women's brigade was formalized. I say it was formalized as its structure had long existed at Mkushi. They fielded other comrades to the positions. Many factors contributed to appointment in any position within the structures. I know three which were the level of education, physical fitness, and maturity/age although there may be others. It was almost independence; buses came to ferry us to Lusaka and we were airlifted to Harare. Because it was now time for campaigns, we stayed with party members at their houses as we were not allowed to go back home for security reasons. We used to gather at Salvation Army Church in Harare and spend the rest of the day singing and waiting for the address and later returning to our parents. This is what we would do as our daily routine. I came back to Bulawayo and returned to Harare.

I also stayed at Sierra assembly point where we would be chosen to be attested into the army or to be demobilized. I came to the Brady barracks where I was attested and integrated into the army. I retired from the army working in the national medical training school. I have always been the director of ceremonies of state functions in the province especially passing out parades, independence, and defence forces day.

PICTURES OF MKUSHI CAMP

Pictures used in this publication were accessed from Zenzo Nkobi Collection kept at Mafela Trust and South African History Archive (SAHA).

Fig 36: (Left): Nikita Mangena addressing women combatants.

Fig 37: (Below): Chief of Staff Ambrose Mutinhiri emphasizing a point to Mkushi Camp women combatants during a parade.

Fig 38: Deputy Camp Commander Sylvester and Sijabuliso JB Gumede in combat attire.

Fig 39: Women combatants singing at Mkushi

CHAPTER 17

'Our broadcast became the vehicle behind indoctrination and massive recruitment'

Jane Ngwenya
(ZAPU Woman Nationalist)

Fig 40: The late Freedom Fighter, ZAPU Female Nationalist and radio broadcaster the late Ms. Jane Lungile Ngwenya. The interview was conducted with the late, Ms. Ngwenya on the 6 February 2021 at Edith Duly in Bulawayo where she resided. Picture source: Accessed from Jane's personal archive.

My name is Jane Lungile Ngwenya. I was born on 15 June 1935, at Buhera, Manicaland. I joined the liberation struggle as a nationalist as I sought to liberate my country from the clutches of colonial repression. I grew up at the height of land invasion by the colonial regime where they used different laws to disenfranchise the black community. More so, we were not seen as a people [blacks]. We were considered lesser humans and some would call us baboons or devil incarnates merely because of our skin colour. Opportunities of employment or privileges were given to the white community or those blacks that were in good books with missionaries.

Issues of inequalities and repression frustrated me and made me determined to join the struggle and fight the system. For me, it was double trouble. Growing up as a girl child, life was never easy and equal. If one wanted to pursue their education, at times the cultural stereotypes would deter then in favour of a boy child. I witnessed it to some of my brilliant friends who failed to pursue their studies, for their families preferred their brothers over them. Besides, it happened to every household as parents would use their meagre resources to fund our education. For me, joining the liberation struggle presented an opportunity to fight the colonial repression and cultural stereotypes that undermined the full participation of women in our society.

From the 1950s to the early 1960s, I then joined the struggle as I became an activist for African National Congress (ANC), National Democratic Party (NDP), and finally Zimbabwe African People's Union (ZAPU). I remember we would be incarcerated for staging demonstrations. One time I was jailed at WhaWha prison with the likes of Joseph Msika and I should think Ruth Chinamano. It was not easy as during the time most leaders of the trade unions and political parties that I interacted with were male-dominated and there were few women.

At some point, my marriage suffered a setback as my husband couldn't tolerate my arrests and activism that sought to empower the black majority. I couldn't be free at home and oppressed everywhere else where I went especially at shops, parks, and other public spheres, I was not free. We parted ways and I became more determined to work for the people of Zimbabwe. At one point, I rose through the ranks and became part of the executive of ZAPU. It was not easy to work with male counterparts as one would be looked down upon or at worst be subjected to unqualified stereotypes. But remember I told you that I was determined to fight the system and the cultural stereotypes that undermined women. With time I blended in and took responsibilities with women like Thenjiwe Lesabe, Nyamurohwa, and other women that joined us later.

Now turning to the role of female combatants, remember I said my name is Jane Ngwenya. I did not have a war name or pseudo name for the simple reason that I did not train or receive military training. I was not a female combatant but a nationalist responsible for the policy direction in the party. To make it simple for you, I joined the liberation struggle as a member of the party. For you to be a nationalist you needed to join the party and be an active member of the party. However, for one to be a ZPRA combatant, they needed to be recruited, trained, deployed, and managed by the command element. While I comment about the female combatant, it is prudent that you understand the context to which I am responding.

Within the liberation phase, as the war intensified, the party had to take a bold decision to include female combatants in recruitment. The decision was that it was also proper to recruit female combatants so that they occupy positions in the rear while male combatants continue at the front. Although there were mixed reactions to whether female recruits will manage to be trained cadres, the decision was adopted.

In that vein, among other responsibilities the party assigned me to be a radio broadcaster, together with John Mbedzi. There were four fundamental reasons why the broadcast was necessary. First, it was to counter the colonial narratives that were broadcast at home to the citizens. In some instances, the colonial regime would misinform the black community as they were also at war to pacify the liberation struggle. Hence it was important to inform the citizens of the developments, successes, and what we hoped to achieve using indigenous languages.

Second, the radio broadcast was necessary to send a message of hope to those in the struggle and those at home. They needed to be given information to soldier on and never to grow weary. It was seen that we needed to account to the masses through radio. Third, and more fundamental, the radio program was used to invite recruits to join the struggle. It was seen as unethical to recruit masses without explaining to them what was pursued, by who, and for what reasons.

We couldn't recruit, they needed to first understand who the war was waged against, and be educated about our black leaders. It is not surprising that all-female combatants in the publication, young as they were, knew about Joshua Nkomo, Jane Ngwenya, and John Mbedzi before meeting them. They need to know who was recruiting them. We couldn't recruit without following best practices, as that would amount to abductions and ZPRA was not a terrorist organization. It was a proper army that followed the procedures of any other liberation army in Africa and beyond.

I broadcast in isiNdebele, English and at times in ChiShona and Mbedzi went further to broadcast in TshiVenda, TjiKalanga, Sesotho, and IsiNdebele. He was talented. Now that the objective was to recruit masses, young and old, it needed us to dramatize our programs so that they would appeal to everyone. I remember, I used to make it clear that, 'Come and join the war, and fight the oppressive colonial system, so that you get a better education. Come and get your gun and you fight'. We packaged it in such a way that whoever would be listening could have that ambition and zeal to fight the system more determined.

At one point I bumped into Nikita Mangena at a corridor in Zimbabwe House and he stopped me and shared a joke, '*Madam Ngwenya kanti amasotsha angitshela ukuthi abantwana bayadana nxa sibanika izigodo zoku-trainer, bathi uJane wabathembisa imibhobho okumele bayisebenzise empini ukudubula amakhiwa*' (Madam Ngwenya, I am told by my instructors that some recruits are now sad because they have been given sticks in place of guns to use for training. I am told they are saying that Jane promised them guns the moment they cross over to the liberation. The guns they shall use to wage a war against the whites). Indeed, we had done progress by recruiting masses that knew what we wanted. I cannot be absolute, but the majority of the recruits knew what was expected of them in the training.

As the war intensified, the war council, which was the highest decision body, constituting of nationalists and military commanders, met and decided to also train female combatants. The decision was not that simple as there were many considerations. The consensus was that trained female combatants were to occupy specific roles at the rear and not in the front and operations. They were meant not to embark on operations and front but to do work in liberated zones across all departments of the party and army. If by any chance you hear a ZPRA female combatant [say] that she went to the front, ask her which area did she operate in, who was her commander? If she answers those questions tell them that they are fat lies, ZPRA did not deploy trained female combatants in the front.

The party and army were consulting us on the idea of training female combatants. Primarily, I was asked as one of the first women who joined the party, which had many male counters. In a way, they wanted to use my experience to come up with a more contextual framework that accommodated a female in their true sense in their gender and female as a female cadre. Joshua Nkomo had to call me that time he was with Dabengwa. At that moment I was with Madam Thaka in the office. Nkomo said,

'MaNgwenya, akelingitshele lithi lifuna sifundise amankazana abe ngamasotsha. Liqinisile sibili. Amankazana ngcono ayefunda ezikolo. Phela bafundiswa ngamajaha abayaziyo into abayenzayo abanye bazakufa besengifika ngisithini ebazalini babo?' (MaNgwenya, are you implying that you are also seconding the view that we train female recruits to be ZPRA cadres. What if they die during the training, for I know that their instructors are seasoned military personnel and they won't lower standards for them. What will I tell their parents if they die in the training?)

I quickly had to tell him [Nkomo] that if other military wings in Africa are doing that, why would ZPRA side-line women. I said it boldly as I knew that I wanted him to understand that while I had joined the war to fight the colonial system, I was also in the quest of fighting the cultural stereotypes. I [am] not saying that Nkomo was resisting it on a cultural basis but he approached the issue in his capacity as a father.

I asserted that when myself and other women joined the struggle there were few women but we managed to blend in. His concern was more to do with physical training and welfare. In 1974, there was a young lady who was called Cecelia Nkomazana. She wanted to join ZPRA and train but she was deterred as at the time females were not allowed. On that day, Mangena and Mazinyane later convinced her [Nkomazana] to join the scholarship program.

Other female nationalists and I continued to persuade other nationalists and military cadres to adopt female recruits as cadres. Another group of women that included Julia Masangweni and Khube Madeya came that same year wanting to join the training, but [were] later sent away on scholarship. However, in 1975 a small number came in as recruits and to be trained. I remember the day, when the news reached us that female combatant recruits have arrived, I was in Vatican Offices with Cephas Cele and said to him, 'Please tell your soldiers never to abuse our female cadres.' I had to be blunt because I had pressured the command element and other nationalists to agree that we also needed female combatants and they needed to be respected, protected and safeguarded by everyone.

When they had trained for at least a month at Mwembeshi, Nkomo and other members of the high command visited them. I was supposed to attend that activity as Joshua would ask me to monitor their welfare now that I had studied issues of social services and welfare, but I was preparing to travel abroad in Cuba. In place of me, a lady called Nyamurohwa went with them. I am told Nkomo had gone there to assess their way of living and tried to persuade them to take up courses but all nine female combatants are said to have refused. On the second encounter, he also sent Dabengwa but they all refused.

I had to politely ask Mangena [about] the progress of female combatants in the training, and he responded that reports he is getting from their instructors are that they are doing well like their male counterparts. In one of the meetings in July 1975, after the Mgagao attack, I said that if women survived then it means they must be trained for those nine showed bravery. From that day, Nkomo marvelled at how the nine female combatants managed to come out of the obstacle and survived an attack. This prompted the massive recruitment of other female recruits for military training between 1975 and 1977. After the training, some were seconded for further military training in various departments of rank and file and others worked as secretaries, camp commanders, intelligence department, security, and in administration.

It was a pleasure to work with them as they were quite disciplined and more determined to work hard in liberating their country. Some would come to the Zimbabwe House and be shown me, and they would say is this the popular Jane we heard on radios back home. To me, it was a confirmation to say we have played our role and hence they needed to take over and work with us not as recruits but as colleagues.

Coming to the issue of abuse and sexuality matter, that subject is still a sensitive issue for many. Few of them would come out to discuss that subject matter as they feel that some people were taking advantage of them. The policy was that in training that had both men and women, the two groups would be staying in separate directions with their facilities and only share dining or kitchen. However, we are talking of young girls who were growing up between 13-17 years and others got themselves in relationships. I remember in the first group of female combatants' report reached us that one got pregnant.

Naturally, she was withdrawn from the training and taken care of at Victory Camp. At Mkushi among the first group, I remember a girl committed suicide after she discovered that a senior instructor was double-crossing her with another. Such things happened. We should at least acknowledge them so that we move on [rather] than to be economical with the truth. Such things happened, and when they did happen, we always voiced out to protect female combatants for we knew that [the] power dynamics between them and their male counterparts were different. We needed to guard against indiscipline in camps.

I end by saying that female combatants looked to us as inspiration. We needed to be exemplary in all our work. They did a wonderful job in their training and assignment execution.

Fig 41: The picture shows members of the Revolutionary Council, individuals identified are Joshua Nkomo, D. Dabengwa, Musarurwa, G. Silundika, C. Cele, A. Ndlovu, F. Makonese and P. Makoni and Jane Ngwenya spotted as the only woman in the picture. The picture used in this publication was accessed from the Zenzo Nkobi Collection kept at Mafela Trust and South African History Archive (SAHA).

CHAPTER 18

'Preaching the ideology of the party and army through music'

Happiness Sibanda
(Light Machine Gun Choir Member)

Fig 42: Freedom Fighter, Happiness Sibanda. She was a member of the Light Machine Gun choir. She and other members of the group entertained and preached the ideology of the party in various camps that they visited. Their music is still very popular in the post-independent state for remembering the bravery of the freedom fighters.

My name is Happiness Sibanda, I was born in 1964 in Beitbridge. I went to primary school at Shashi and later Limpopo. While growing we heard stories of the brutality of white people against blacks. Our parents spoke of how they were treated at workplaces and were complaining about how they were discriminated against in some public spaces. Naturally, what is discussed at home by parents influences how you think and do things. I also remember them talking about Joshua Nkomo, that he and ZAPU sought to emancipate the nation and the blacks against colonialism. I should emphasize that I was very young by then. I definitely was not politically conscious. Growing up at Shashi, my sister and I took turns to herd livestock. While herding our livestock, we would be confronted by people asking for some directions to cross over Botswana.

That time I did not know where they were going. Little did we know that they were going to join the struggles. At some point, guerrillas would ask us the whereabouts of the whites and innocently we would tell them. We did not know that they were guerrillas who had come to do a reconnaissance. We would tell them every information that they needed. We were innocent.

By 1976, there was a radio broadcaster who worked with Jane Lungile Ngwenya inviting people to join the struggle. He was called John Mbedzi.[23] He would broadcast using Venda language urging people to join the struggle that if we crossed and joined the struggle in Zambia, liberators shall come back and be given farms and mines. Both of them would dramatize their program as if they were watching you.

In January 1977 while I had taken the livestock to drink water by the river, a tall man who was wearing a very long jacket approached and greeted me. While I was about to drift away from him, he told me to stop and not to run away. I realized that there was something bulgy on his back, more of a stick or a gun. Possibly it was a gun! The man asked me whether I knew John Mbedzi - the radio broadcaster, and I said I knew him as a broadcaster. He then said that he wanted to take [me] to Mbedzi in Zambia since I have confirmed that I knew him. I quickly called my sister Nelly who was nearby and told him that what we usually hear on-air had finally come, that we go to Zambia as we used to hear the broadcast. I told her (my sister) that they wanted to go with us to meet up with Mbedzi.

Imagine, there and there we left all the livestock and followed the man who had approached me. At that time, I went following them with bare feet without putting on shoes. We followed the guerrilla as they headed into the Shashi Mountain. We stayed there for some time while they were monitoring the movement of the white officers. While they were still at the top of the mountain, they changed their clothes and climbed down the mountain to the nearby shops. I think this was done to hide their identity. They went there to look for bread. When they came, they gave us bread and we waited for a while before we left. We left at dusk when it was almost dark.

When we got to Shashi, the river was full to the brim as you would imagine, that it was early January - the rainy season. As a young girl, I tried crossing but I almost drowned. I was saved by that guerrilla that approached me and invited me to join the struggle. He took me and put me onto his shoulders and made me cross over. We managed to cross the river and moved a bit to the nearby homesteads in Botswana. This is where we slept that night. Early morning, we woke up and started walking in an unknown direction. This time our number had increased as we were joined by others that were recruited like us. We walked quite a long way and remember I was barefooted without any sandals or shoes. I

---

[23]Mr. John Mbedzi was a ZAPU broadcaster based at Lusaka in Zambia who worked with Ms. Jane Ngwenya and broadcast in Sesotho, TshiVenda, IsiNdebele and ChiShona. His program was widely heard inside Zimbabwe, inviting citizens to join the struggle.

114

got tired as I was not used to such, and worse I was only 13 years old. After walking a long journey, a big truck only intercepted us after some time and took us to Selibe-Phikwe.

At Selibe-Phikwe, we stayed at the prison cells and had a lifestyle that was not so different from prisoners. What they ate and the water that they used to bath was all the same. The difference was that they were serving their sentences and we were seeking the quest to liberate our country. At the prison we stayed there without any activity. I can't remember how many months we stayed there. One day as we were there, we were told that we are to move to Zambia. A big airplane came and pick us up.

I was very happy as this was my first experience to board a plane. We flew to Lusaka, Zambia and proceeded to Victory Camp. In our group I was the youngest girl, who everyone was marvelling because of the size and age. We slept at a place called Big Bhawa, although we got harassed by lice. We used to call the lice comrade. It became more interesting in that when you killed one today within minutes another one will harass you. [We had] small legumes that appeared like beans but it was called *umtshatshatsha*. We ended up not killing the [lice] and called it comrade as it became a permanent feature in our life time at VC. Even the type of food was terrible. Everyday was a struggle.

At VC, ZPRA officials did not care about your age whether you were young or old - you will all be taken through a similar process, which was very painful. We woke up early morning in our companies to do a toyi-toyi coupled with road runs. Imagine at 13 years I used to do all that. The painful experience! At VC, I also remember there were already accomplished female combatants who had completed their training. There was Jane, Audrey, Constance and Bvundzai.

At times you would go and bath but as soon as the whistle is blown, you would then be forced to abandon bathing and run to the next activity as per the order. We could be given oversized combat gear that we called 'rice' you would be told to wear it as it was. This meant that one had to find ways of making it fit in a manner that you felt comfortable in it. You would even be given different sizes of shoes and have to wear [them]. What else could we have done? Absolutely nothing!

That lifestyle was very painful. I was the youngest in that camp with no peers of my age mates. My age mates only came when the first group of women were taken to be trained at Mkushi camp. That is the time when VC assumed the status of a refugee camp. It became a refugee camp after the transition.

By 1978, while at VC, we began to question whether the war was really going to end. We began to lose hope of whether we were actually going to get independence or what? We questioned whether Ian Smith was prepared to cede power or we were fighting a cat like system with many lives? We got mixed feelings whether the war, was it going to end or we were all going to die in

Zambia and never to return home to see our parents once more? One day we decided to gather and chant seeking answers to those questions and more importantly entertaining ourselves while telling a story of what we think of the war, and its end game. This was the birth of the Light Machine Gun choir which assumed a status of preaching the ideology of the party, documenting our history, visualize our aspirations and, more importantly, to entertain combatants in various ZPRA camps. At that time, the group comprised of twenty-five members that is fifteen males and ten females. I am referring to the gender component as females and males, not men and women, for we were very young by then.

I have to emphasize to say the primary aim to form the choir was to sing and entertain others in the camp. But however, it later assumed a charge to work with the ZPRA commissar, who was called Swalu [Saul] Nare, and hence it ended up entertaining, preaching the ideology of the party/army, and telling a story of the liberation struggle.

It then became the main vocal of the party, going to every camp in Nampundwe, Freedom Camp and Zimbabwe House, entertaining people but telling a story of the war situation and bringing hope to the people. I have to make it clear that it preached the ideology of the party, working closely with the then commissar Nare, who would tell us different stories of what was happening elsewhere, back at home or in other training camps. We told a story using such stories drawn from the stories of our commissar. No wonder why one cannot separate Nare and the Light Machine Gun. The two are inseparable. He was the leader. I remember sometime we visited the Zimbabwe House, which was the headquarters of the party, and its military wing in Zambia. We had gone there to sing and entertain the delegates while giving people hope and telling the story.

I remember when Freedom camp was bombed, we went to identify bodies and pick some of them for burial. Little did we know that Mkushi was also targeted. After those incidents a song was composed that went like, 'Laphuma lababahle (You were as beautiful as you were) imvelo yonke yayinhle (Even the nature was as beautiful as you were).'

The above song aimed at giving hope to the combatants. It underscored the fact that they had all done their great initiative to cross from various areas to fight a colonial system which was very heinous. In the above song, you will realize that we also ridiculed the colonial government that they had shown cowardice together with Bishop Abel Muzorerwa. Our songs were composed in such a way that sought to comfort survivors, casualties and preach the ideology of the party.

We were never partisan or divisive in our approach. We sang in different languages to reflect the fact that ZAPU-ZPRA was never tribal and neither did it see ZANU-ZANLA as a competitor but as a revolutionary force in achieving the objective of ZAPU-ZPRA which was to liberate Zimbabwe and her people. That's why you would hear songs like, *Vana vakatiza and Tinotenda vaNkomo nhavaMugabe*. These songs were sung in the ChiShona language which meant that our war was never tribal nor regional as our detractors would want to illustrate. Many will give you an impression that ZAPU-ZPRA was of the Ndebele, no! It was for everyone. Its mischievous for one to regionalize the party that had a national character and outlook.

There were other songs which were composed to position and champion our leaders as capable of leading the independent Zimbabwe. One song that comes to mind that speaks to this fact went like, *Siyabonga abakhokheli ababuya lelizwe leZimbabwe* (We appreciate the work that was done by our leaders). I want to emphasize that Nkomo made it in black and white that we are not approaching the liberation in a divided front. Hence to us, we would sing and include ZANU-ZANLA, for the war was meant to benefit the people of Zimbabwe. Even if we had lost the elections, Nkomo made it clear that we needed to accept defeat and move on. Using that framework, our songs remain relevant as they were composed with the message of hope and unity. Also, there were other songs that were composed for Nkomo so that he would not grow weary in leading the revolution. Songs like, *Ilitshe likaNkomo limbombozile, and Sizogijima sihlangabeza uNkomo (*We shall run and embrace our leader Joshua Nkomo) among others.

There were other songs like; *Guerrilla ilanga litshonile* (Guerrilla remember dusk), *Itoyi toyi yikuzelula amathambo* (Toyi-toyi is just an exercise.). Such songs were meant to remind the guerrillas of the objective of why they joined the struggle, and more importantly to embrace challenges as they come, as they were bound to happen. Songs we sang in various camps were not only preaching the ideology and for entertainment but as time went on, they assume a state of giving morale and energy to guerrillas. Those that sustained injuries along the way were comforted by the same songs that we sang.

In fact, if you really listen to our songs, they were composed in such a way that they spoke to individuals back at home to collaborate and support those in the liberation struggle, give morale to the guerrillas and comforted those who had grown weary or got injured along [the way]. Those back home knew our songs. Above all, songs immortalized those who would die along the way that their sacrifice shall never be forgotten. No wonder why, our songs are still very relevant in the current context.   For example, there is a song *Sijabule namuhlanje sithethe iZimbabwe* (We are very happy today, that as the black majority we have regained control of our country Zimbabwe). It speaks to our teaching and ideology that even if we in ZAPU then lost elections, the basis is that our country was now at the hands of the black majority. This was the important thing! I know many people know this one that goes like *Emoyeni kwakubuhlungu*! (It is painful in our spirits and hearts).

I have to correct a misconception that our songs were sung during pungwes. We never conducted pungwe outreaches. We sang these songs in ZPRA camps and never held any pungwes. I cannot speak wholly for those that went to some operations but all I know is that they never held any pungwes to make people

117

sing. Besides where were the people? We were in Zambia not at home, and even then ZPRA guerrillas did not hold pungwes at home for we did not need to mobilize citizens but to collaborate with them while fighting with the enemy.

When we returned back home, we sang songs like *Sangena eZimbabwe (We have entered Zimbabwe once more), Sijabule namhlanje sithethe iZimbabwe* (We are finally happy for we have taken back our country into the hands of the black majority).

After independence, we returned home. Remember, I said, a chosen few were requested to accompany Joshua Nkomo back to the then Southern Rhodesia, now Zimbabwe. In my capacity as the member of the LMG I came back to Zimbabwe by plane which landed at Harare together with other trained female combatants from Mkushi. Upon arrival we were given foster parents as we were not allowed to return to our real homes which we grew up in for other security considerations. Besides, the party was still preparing for the 1980 general elections. As such, each person was then allocated foster parents and I was allocated to stay with Joshua Nkomo at Number 6.

I stayed with the Nkomo family and I remember at some point Nkomo asked me where I wanted to enroll for my education. I almost said I wanted to go to Mzilikazi High School but I went silent. I stayed there for some time, and when other refugees came from FC by train and I think they landed at Luveve to prepare their enrollment back to school. However, I was made to join other trained female combatants at Sierra camp in Gweru. That's where I received my demobilization. At Sierra Camp, I was received by the camp commander who was Sigoge-Maphala. She was very tall and very patient. As some were chosen to join the army, nursing, and teaching among other things. I decided to go back to school and enrolled as a student at Fatima High School.

Joshua Nkomo released me to join others at Fatima. I did my Form 1-4, but I failed to come up with good grades. I retook my studies at Foundation College in Bulawayo. I should state that young people would laugh at us as we were now learning with them as old as we were. I then passed and proceeded to do a diploma in teaching with United College of Education. The same was true as we learnt with young people at college and I was now a bit old. I did not give up as I knew I was passionate but I was only disadvantaged by my background. I graduated and went on to teach one month at Chithekani Primary and later at Robert Sinyoka. I, however, approached the then governor, the late Mr. Welshman Mabhena, and requested that I so wished to teach at the CBD so as to improve my skills. I explained to him that I needed to improve a lot of skills now that I spent most of my time in the bush - the liberation struggle. I was then moved to teach at Milton Junior and since then I have never moved from there and will retire this year from teaching.

I should also state this, that because of the Unity Accord, I joined the mainstream politics as an active member of Zanu PF and served in various portfolios in

Matabeleland. At some point, I served as a councillor and currently I am the secretary of finance for the veterans of the liberation struggle in Matabeleland. I am married to Mr. Jimmy Sibanda and have four children.

SIJABULE NAMHLANJE
(We are very happy today)

Sijabule namhlanje is a song which was sung by the Light Machine Gun Choir. It is from this song that this publication used one of the lyrics, *Yithi Laba* as its title. The song was transcribed from the original song of the Light Machine Gun-Choir accessed from the internet. The author selected the lyrics of the song. Transcribed lyrics have been presented in a linear order as sung and not in a standard musical annotation.

Sijabule namhlanje

We're happy today
(*English loose translation*)

Sijabule namhlanje	We're happy today
Sithethe iZimbabwe	We've won Zimbabwe.
Sijabule namhlanje	We're happy today
Sithethe iZimbabwe	We've won Zimbabwe.

Yithi laba— esasingekho
Yithi laba— esasingekho
Yithi laba— abantwabenu,
esasithiwa singagandanga
esasithiwa singamathororo

This is us, who've away
This is us, who've away
This is us, your children
Who were known as guerrillas
Who were labelled terrorists.

Wonke amaqhawe aseZimbabwe,
Ababethiwa ngamagandanga,
Ababethiwa ngamathororo.

All the heroes and heroines
Who were known as guerrillas
Who were labelled terrorists.

Yiy' oyibona namhla
Yon' iZimbabwe.
Yiy' oyibona namhla
Yon' iZimbabwe.
Namuhla siyithethe ikhululekile
Namuhla siyithethe ikhululekile
Namuhla siyithethe ngeyethu sonke.
Namuhla siyithethe ngeyethu sonke.

This is it that you see today
The Zimbabwe
This is it that you see today
The Zimbabwe
Today, we've won it—it's free
Today, we've won it—it's free
Today, we've won it—it's for us all!
Today, we've won it—it's for us all!

Namuhla bayothini?
Namuhla bayothini?
Sesitheth' iZimbabwe!
Sesitheth' iZimbabwe!

Today, what will they say?
Today, what will they say?
We've won Zimbabwe!
We've won Zimbabwe!

CHAPTER 19

'Caught in between'

Maretha Dube

Fig 43: War Collaborator Maretha Dube who was part of the Manama group and returned home after her father intercepted her on their way to Zambia. She then worked closely with the freedom fighters as a war collaborator. After the war she worked for the Ministry of Health as a nurse aide. She later trained as a school teacher before rising to the position of a lecture. She is currently working as a Language Research Assistant at the Midlands state University.

My name is Maretha Dube nee Mazhale. I grew up in Gwanda Maditlou village under Chief Gungwe. Growing up I was known as Kerina Mazhale. I got the name Maretha later. I attended Gungwe and Ntepe Primary School. When I went to Manama Secondary School for form 1 in 1977 things turned for the unexpected. What I thought would be part of my education turned out to be some kind of involvement in the liberation struggle. It was around 6pm when the bell rung. Senior students told us it was supper time. We rushed to the dinning hall. Before we got to the hall, we found a large group of students grouped under a tree. There was this loud and harsh voice from a man who was asking questions. As we wondered what was happening, we realized that it was members of ZPRA forces. They had grouped students and asking questions in Ndebele. Precisely, he was asking:

"*Kuyini lokhu?*" (What's this?)

Yisikolo (It's a school)

Lenzani (What are you doing?)

Siyafunda (We're learning)

Lifundani (What are you learning?)

Amabhuku (Books)

Ukuthi lenzeni ngamabhuku (What do you intend to do with books?)

Ukuthi sithuthukise ilizwe lethu (So that we develop our country)

At that point he said "Bloody shit. *Linika uSmith imali ngeschool fees imali yokuthi athenge inhlamvu sokusibulala* (You are giving Smith money through school fees so that he can buy bullets to kill us?

Hayi lathi sasivele sifuna ukuyempini (No. We actually wat to join the war)

Then what have you been waiting for?

"*Ukuthi izikolo zivulwe* (So that schools could open)

There was no negotiation after that.

We started moving in a direction I I had no clue of. I was identified as one of the youngest learners at Manama. They kept checking on us the small ones saying, *Bangaphi labana abantwana abancane* (Where are those kids). We went through Mapate and Halisupi. By then I had lost my shoes. They went to get food from Mr Jabhi's shop. They remembered I had lost my shoes and they brought me new shoes from his shop. I was with my cousin from my maternal aunt and we held hands as we walked because I was young and needed help to keep up. Someone suddenly sperated our hands saying, *"Yindaba lihamba libambene? Lifuna ukubaleka"* (Why are you holding hands? You want to run away.

By dawn we were at Shashe River. That is when I realized that we were going to Botswana. One of the popular people we had with us was our Headmaster Mr Glory Makwati and a student named Naledi Kukubele. As soon as we crossed river Shashe we saw some aeroplanes hovering above us. At that point we realized that Mr Makwati had disappeared.

"*Ungaphi umdala lwana*" (Where is that man). I later learnt that he had gone back home to our paternal grandmother. My grandmother asked him,

121

"*Umntwana umtshiye ngaphi?*" (Where did you leave our baby?)

The ZPRA forces were angry that he had gone back and he was carrying a cash box with him. When we had crossed Shashe nearing Gobajango, the ZPRA forces no longer had guns. We were instructed to tell the villagers that we were not abducted but had come at our free will. Some Tswana women were crying asking what our parents were saying.

At Gobajango we were taken to a homestead where we were fed. From there we waited for open trucks to ferry us It was raining and we got soaked. We were taken to the refugee camp and we were addressed on the second day. They told us precisely that;

"*Angithi lizwile ukuthi uSmith uthumele amabhasi ukuthi abazali bezolithatha. Akulamuntu okumele abuyele. Ozabuyela sizambona mhla sithatha ilizwe.*

Naledi Kukubele was interviewed by journalists. She encouraged us not to go back home because some had this courage to proceed. We felt encourage not to go back home. We were caught in between when our parents came and asked "*uyahamba yini*" (Are you going?). And they only accepted the first answer. You were not allowed to change once you had answered. My father asked and I said yes, I am going. What I observed was that the busses were virtually empty as many refused to go back home.

My father worked as an accounts clerk in some retail shops. Upon return from Botswana, my father retired and came home to stay with us. We were later told that he resigned from work so that he could be home with us and protect his children. He quit his job and my education was affected as I could not proceed with education because there were threats that those who are sending kids to schools would be dealt with after the war. Parents were afraid to send their children off to school.

As all that happened, I think the spirit of liberation had gotten the better of me, I became the chairperson of the youth wing. Our role was to mobilize each other and be part of the struggle and assist the fighters in the best way we could. Our role was to raise funds and buy cigarettes while parents bought bigger stuff. We had a roster for cooking and feeding the fighters. It was not easy but we got used to it and it became part of our lives. I remember my first encounter with them after my return, I met them on my way from the fields. I was asked to go and call my parents. We then began cooking and washing for them.

We were used to the sound of bus engines as they would come to our village. On this particular Sunday we heard familiar sound and assumed it was the busses not knowing it was the Rhodesian army trucks.

One thing I will never forget is the Ndungwane battle which was a clash between the ZPRA forces and Rhodesian army. We were expected to have information as the youth. When the fighters came the next day, they wanted to know from us of the incident involving gunshots but we had no information. They said they expected us to have the information because they trusted us. They later threatened us saying they want substantial information the following day. Coincidentally, these were the guys in the Manama group. As the chairperson, the following day I took my bike and cycled to Ndungwane to gather intelligence. On the way I met the army trucks. I had been instructed by the fighters to bring their kit bags. My brother stopped me from executing the tasks and said the task was too big for me. There was a clash and I was almost caught in the crossfire. When I got home after sunset, I found people gathered at home worried that I was probably killed in the clashes. That had become very common.

These were things that happened but most importantly my education was disturbed.

After the war a relative took me to Bulawayo where I studied for a certificate at the Red Cross. After that I became e a nurse aide for 9 years. I was enrolled for evening part time studies. It took me some years took acquire 5 O levels. I later trained as a teacher and furthered my studies towards a Bachelor's Degree, became a college lecturer now I am a researcher at a university. This is how I was involved in the liberation struggle and how it affected my education.

I cannot remember any other students that returned from Botswana besides Naledi Kukubele, P K *Maplanka* Mthombeni and a few others who had proceeded to the war. I particularly remember one my classmates, Ezra Wadega, and how I envied them after the war when he had joined the army while I was suffering and trapped in poverty. Sometimes I would ask myself what could have become of me had I proceeded to the war or continued with my education. I probably could have gone far or maybe I could have died of other war related ailments, but also, I believe it was all God's plan.

CHAPTER 20

'Accounting for the absence, gaps and silences of ZPRA's women combatants in the broad liberation historiography'

Zephaniah Nkomo
(Former Director of Mafela Trust)

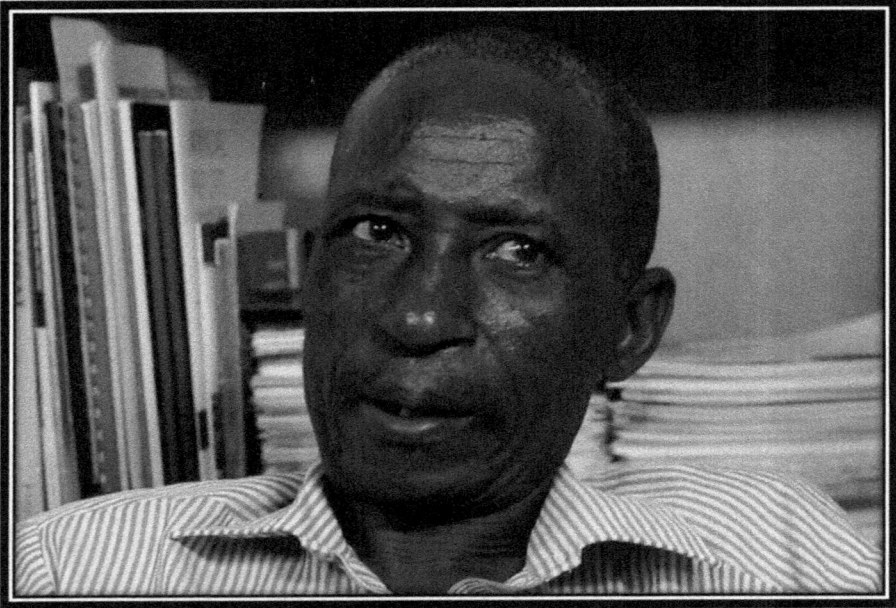

Fig 44: The late Freedom Fighter, Mr. Zephaniah Nkomo. At the time of his death, Nkomo was the National Director of Mafela Trust, a repository organization that was formed to document and write the history of ZAPU/ZPRA as well as spearhead peacebuilding programs in communities. In the liberation struggle, he received security training and later advanced in police and security training at Lilayi Police Training in Zambia. He later served in various security departments in ZAPU-ZPRA. The interview was conducted with Mr Zephaniah Nkomo six months before his death.

The gaps and silences of the role of honour of trained Zimbabwe People's Revolutionary Army (ZPRA) women during the liberation struggle cannot be treated in isolation with the gaps and silences that ZAPU and her military wing ZPRA encountered in post-independence Zimbabwe.

Understand the fact that victors are the writers of the history and as victors of the 1980 elections, ZANU PF led government forgot about ZAPU and ZPRA and wrote a celebrated history which gave glory and positioned them as the only party that went into the war. This was in sync with their ploy of enacting one party state and everything of ZAPU or ZPRA was annihilated and considered dangerous, including their history.

Secondly, the history of ZAPU and ZPRA never found space in the national memory as it has to be said that ZANU PF looted the documents and archives of the former in 1982–1987 and they were never recovered. Looting was done to our archives so that we won't be able to write our history as what we had was considered as disturbing truth versus what they had. That's why you find our history is not fully appearing. Over the years we have tried to rebuild our archives through research work.

The gaps that may be found in various state institutional sectors that include Ministry of Education, Ministry of Information, Ministry of Home Affairs, particularly National Archives, Museum and Monuments, among other things are a result of deliberate side-lining of this movement of ZAPU and its military wing ZPRA, the reason was that there is too much disturbing truth about what we all have in telling the story of the liberation to the nationBeacuse of their power they wrote the history in the way how they wanted up to the point in which they side-line the history of ZAPU and ZPRA. Nationalist historiography required us both ZANU and ZAPU to have an equal share of telling our stories so as to champion nation building and the culture of truth telling. But Robert Mugabe did the opposite!

During the Gukurahundi atrocities, our liberation heroes and heroines were reduced to mere historical actors [rather] than liberators. Some were called snakes, dissidents, murderers and all sorts of names which naturally made a structural mode of side-lining members of ZAPU or ZPRA from history. From those atrocities often spoken about, some went into hiding and never wanted to participate in any national projects. This included ZPRA's female combatants and women nationalists at large. Remember this was a strategy of also discouraging our members as it intimidated them. Gukurahundi was a strategy to smear ZAPU or ZPRA that they should not revolt against ZANU PF-led government.

While a lot has been written about male nationalists and other distinguished ZPRA guerrillas, the aspect of trained ZPRA women combatants is still unknown. Gaps may be quite apparent; we have the sector which looks into the role which was played by women during the liberation struggle and of which that sector has not been adequately dealt with. There are several reasons why, apart from the deliberate side-lining of ZAPU-ZPRA's history into national memory and the history of the liberation struggle. There were challenges presented to us in collecting the biographies and liberation contribution of women who went to war.

These are people who were part of the liberation struggle and played quite a significant role, which I have to state. Women had a very critical role in the struggle but when we decided to document their role, women in most cases were subjected, probably I think by the nature of their standing, women became submissive to patriarchal values and construct. A lot got missed out as they did not show up in cooperating with the documenting process of the liberation struggle.

For example, they were not left deliberately but the position when coming into the country in 1980, it was a moment that guerrillas were to be reintegrated into the civil society and civil society life. We are talking of building of families, and marriage among other things.

As such female combatants were looking for opportunities to build up their own families. A lot of women were not married to their male counterparts who were freedom fighters but were now married to civilian men. Hence such women, who later married civilians, ended up reframing and adjusting behavioural patterns [of] their past and decided not to take part in any history writing projects that sought to document the history of their party. This made it impossible for researchers to document them, hence that's the reason why there are gaps in the role played by women.

Thirdly, others decided to cut ties with their liberation past because of the harassment and torture they underwent during the building of the unified army which is known as the Army integration and during the Gukurahundi period. Being known as a ZPRA combatant attracted one harassment, intimidation or at worst murder. Some female combatants who were integrated into the new military formation were bold enough and withstood the heat and sailed through while subjected to low ranks, intimidated and labelled sell-outs. Others ended up coming up with new identities so as to cope with the new trends of survival during a very difficult period. This also made it difficult to identify women and document their contribution. Such situations kept them away from activities that would give focus on them.

In the few publications that highlight the history of ZAPU or ZPRA researchers prefer to discuss episodes of nationalist veterans or profiles of the high command. This is because major liberation episodes revolved around the male counterparts hence women are not given limelight in the discussion. The fact that the major gold rush for researchers is that they seek to document and chronicle the battles, encounters and major operations - such battles, encounters and operations were made up of male counterparts as ZPRA did not deploy female guerrillas to the front. Women did not participate in such frontline episodes and hence their back-room contribution in those battles is not told. Worse-still, years into independence Zimbabwe still has no street named after ZPRA female combatants. You have streets and building that are named after their male counter parts.

In some instances, researchers prefer to discuss the stories of women who joined the struggle in 1964 during the initial formation of ZAPU and forget to trail the role of women up to 1980. It is worth noting that some prefer profiling women who worked closely with the members of the high command or the spouses or relatives of those that were in the command. Those who were not related to members of the high command tend to be left out. Documentation has its own politics as it is a researcher who choses what to write and omit!

126

PICTURES OF TRAINED WOMEN COMBATANTS

Pictures used in this publication were accessed from Zenzo Nkobi Collection kept at Mafela Trust and South African History Archive (SAHA).

Fig 45: ZPRA women's brigade marching at the Castle Arms Parade in Bulawayo.

Fig 46: Trained ZPRA women and men cadres with the Commander-in-Chief, Dr. Joshua Nkomo.

CHAPTER 21

'None of them died during the attack: For they were trained!'

Stanford Moyo
(ZPRA cadre who trained with women at Morogoro)

Fig 47: Freedom Fighter, Mr. Stanford Moyo, who trained with the first group of women combatants at Mwembeshi, Mgagao, and Morogoro before he undertaking various military operations.

My name is Stanford Peace Moyo. My war name which I was given in Nampundwe was Lloyd Zvananewako, but during operations in Lupane I was then called Mabhikwa. At Inyathi and Silobela operations I was either called Vumabalanda or Khumalo. You need to understand that war naming was not static it kept on changing based on the gravity of assignment as we thrived to erase trends of identification by the system. Before I narrate my training with the first group of female combatants that we trained with, it is prudent to narrate my background.

I was born in 1955 at Antelope Mine Hospital of Matobo district. I went to Chewondo Primary School up to standard three and later repeated the level at

Lingwe Primary School. At Lingwe that was 1970, I was among the students that pioneered into grade 7 after the authorities had restructured the education system thereby disregarding the standard system.

I joined the liberation struggle from South Africa and crossed to Botswana. We arrived at Mafikeng, Botswana and met six other friends who we were staying with in South Africa. As a group of eight we moved and began by going to the nearby police station and they directed us to go to the maximum prison where those who intended to join the war were kept. We moved in that group and approached the maximum prison. While at the entrance, the prison wardens ran away as they saw us and the other group that was coming behind us. That was January 1975, at 02.00am.

We thought that they had run away, alas they came in a different direction now in big numbers. They asked us where we [were] going and our motive, and we told them that we were going to Francistown to join the war. We were taken in, and given cells to stay in. Inside the prison we met guys that had run away from the University of Zimbabwe, then University of Rhodesia. These are the guys who were contemporaries of Christopher Mutsvanga, but they came to Botswana and Mutsvanga had joined the war on the other side of Mozambique.

Here we were in the prison cells with the learned and speaking the same language of pursuing war. We stayed there since January to July, at some point I thought I would never see my parents. Thoughts of regrets started to knock in as I was disappointed by the type of food we ate; we would eat porridge early morning - instead I remembered how well I ate as a cook in South Africa. Even in the midst of regret we couldn't run away. We stayed there up to July and the influence of those that were learned made us love the idea of joining the struggle as we collectively shared experiences of the colonial experience. We ended up liking the idea.

We moved to Francistown maximum prison. This time we met different colleagues from SWAPO, and Umkhonto we Sizwe. At Francistown, Dumiso Dabengwa came through and we were moved to Zambia at Nampundwe Camp. The camp was a transit camp with no training and all. However, by March 1976 we were moved to Mwembeshi training centre. This is the time I saw nine female recruits who had come to train with us.

At Mwembeshi we stayed as from March to end of May if am not mistaken. Training started there and already I was put in the same section with my homeboys Brighton, Single and seven female recruits. These were Belinda, Jane, Gladys, Constance, Audrey, Vhunzai and I think Grace. I seem to be forgetting others that joined other sections. Our instructors, that included Sam Madondo, Stanley Doko, Madzibaba and Busobenyoka, underscored that they were not only training males or females but whole ZPRA soldiers. There was no segregation. They exerted the same pressure to everyone. We all woke up to toyi-toyi, train physically, do judo, and attend lessons. We did all the training as one without segregation based on gender. We were pursuing war, not issues of discrimination. I remember one time when we had assembled ready for lessons, Stanley Nleya once said, 'we are ZPRA cadres not males or females' he was always reminding us to accommodate each other.

One time Eddie Sigoge took us through the obstacle training, which everyone was supposed to come out of the obstacle and underneath that they were releasing live bullets that in the event one fell down, you were automatically going to be hit hard, either injured or die on the spot. I remember all males started the activity and they completed. In my section, six females followed and they did exceptionally. Then there was this one called Gladys. She was huge and big. We all thought she was going to be hit but the bullet as she tried her way out of the obstacle. In fact, Sigoge marveled and passed a comment that she did well. Sigoge was very tough and never compromised standards, like Gagisa. This shows you that they were training soldiers not a segregation of males or females.

The arrangement in which we stayed at Mwembeshi was such that female cadres had their toilets in the opposite directions of those of their male counterparts. This was done to avoid the problem of indiscipline. Men had their own toilets the opposite direction far away from females. They stayed in one tent now that they were very few in numbers. Socially, you know what happens when males and females meet.

Such happened, but relationships were discouraged and it was easy to note who had done what when and to who, now that female numbers were very few. Naturally, male counterparts wanted to spend more time with female cadres for obvious reasons but I repeat that such was discouraged as we were pursuing war and not pleasures. There are times when one felt affection towards one of the ladies but discipline naturally discouraged you from embarking on such. I remember two female cadres were withdrawn from the training after they had been found to be pregnant. The issue was attended by Nikita Mangena as they intended to set the record straight. Mangena was no nonsense and so had been Lookout Masuku!

I do not rule out your fact on issues of sexual encounters, perhaps it did happen because for them to be pregnant it did not happen the biblical manner of Mary and the angel Gabriel. However, ZPRA had a strong system of discipline and secrecy. That's why you will interview all women who went to war, they will disclose everything but nothing about cases of relationships, inappropriate associations, rape or sexual offenses. It's still a classified factor as some of the perpetrators are still there and it is highly possible that many of them are very powerful individuals in the society. I know of some incidents, but as ZPRA cadres we were taught to swallow the painful experience and only share what is convenient lest we destroy individuals or defame others. This explains why ZPRA did not deploy females in the front for two fundamental points. First, deploying them was going to bring confusion and internal fights. Imagine deployment in the front and you have to carry out your operation in the middle of the bush. After that you wait for the signal. Between the time of end of operation and waiting for the signal what else would you do? You will end up doing the obvious [he laughs], sleeping together and forgetting the primary objective.

Second, when there is a female factor, it was natural that men will end up fighting for them and abandon the major objective hence the enemy would do as they please. I remember during the training at Mwembeshi we used to compete for us to be recognized. I personally liked one of them, which I would not mention by name, but well I ended up concentrating on the training as I saw I stood no chance. Zambians also liked the company of these women combatants.

When we moved to Mgagao under Zimbabwe People's Army (ZIPA), we moved together with the same female cadres and maintained our sections and companies. Our company collaborated with the other company from ZANLA called Daburamanzi. I remember one time, during our first days, ZANLA guys marveled at the manner in which our female cadres did physical training. It was not as if they had started training with us but we used to train as ZPRA doing our military drills while they were watching us.

They got intimidated by the manner in which our females did all the judo, physical and gun assembly. I remember when the shooting started in Mgagao I had gone out to give my homeboys food in one of the tents. As I was out, I heard a loud bang of gun shootings at the dining hall and this was terrible. The shooting started when there was shortage of food as some of our colleagues from ZPRA, who were roughly seven, are said to have [been] denied food that same day. This then sparked the crisis. But I guess there were other underlying problems in the high command element that influenced such differences that are blown out of proportion.

We ran away from the obstacle, including the female cadres. What I did as a male, they all did as females who were equally trained like us as they evaded the obstacle. I do not think any of them died in the scenario which makes it clear that they were soldiers. I recall one of them who I am forgetting the name, who was the first person to crawl and roll down when we were avoiding to cross the main road. It was out of bravery that she led the way. The long and short of it - they did wonders in the midst of the crisis. No wonder they were all nominated to be instructors of other training camps in Mkushi and Mwembeshi. This explains why Smith later targeted female cadres in Mkushi as he had no doubt that if ZPRA continued training women it was going to be hard to destroy ZPRA.

CHAPTER 22

'We trained soldiers. We all gave them the same and similar training!'

Stanley '*Doko*' Gagisa Nleya
(Former ZPRA's senior military instructor)

Picture source: The Chronicle Newspaper (21-06-20).

Fig 48: The late Freedom Fighter, Mr. Stanley Nleya, who was the senior military instructor of both ZPRA female and male combatants. As an instructor, he also went for various military operations at home in Zimbabwe and beyond in search of liberation. He assumed special assignments within the rank and file of ZPRA. This interview was conducted with him on 20 July 2019, before he passed away.

My name is Stanley Nleya from Masendu, Bulilima District of Matabeleland South. My war name was Elish Gagisa but some continued to call me Doko even in the post-colonial period. I joined the war in 1968 when I abandoned my education to join the war.

I left for the liberation war with two other friends of mine. Their names were Elias Ndlovu and Cornelius Dube. We left Plumtree area and crossed Botswana border and to Francistown to a refugee camp that was known as White House. In that refugee camp I met other people like Kelly Malaba, and Richard Gedi Dube. I stayed there for about six months. We were later flown to Zambia to Albert Luthuli Camp which was also a facility for our colleagues from the African

National Congress (ANC) and its military wing Umkhonto Wesizwe. We shared a lot with Umkhonto Wesizwe in terms of operations and campaigns. In 1969, we were moved for military training in Morogoro Tanzania. I trained with people like the late Rtd Col. Masala Sibanda, the late Rtd Major Jevan Maseko, Rtd Brig. Abel Mazinyane, Rtd. Brig. Tshile Nleya and late Rtd Col. Eddie Sigoge. We completed our training after an intense nine months. Upon completing the training, I was chosen to be a military instructor together with others like Jevan Maseko, Tshile Nleya, Eddie Sigoge and Elias Ndlovu.

There was re-organizing phase of ZAPU and ZPRA after a major 'crisis': in that meeting[24] of re-organizing, major appointments were done where Rogers Alfred Nikita Mangena was made chief of staff as the rank of commander was reserved for the party leader Joshua Nkomo who was in prison at that time. Mangena only became commander when Nkomo got the title of supreme commander.

Below Mangena as chief of staff was Lookout Masuku who was political commissar. Cephas Cele came in as chief of training, and Report Phelekezela Mphoko became chief of logistics. The chief of intelligence Gordon Munyanyi, was also responsible for communications and reconnaissance. The chief of operations was John Dube whose real name was Charles Ngwenya while Dumiso Dabengwa was the secretary of the Revolutionary Council.

In that meeting there was the drafting of the Proxy Document, which for the sake of this interview I will mention that it established the department of training and personnel, which I was assigned under as a military instructor. This department of training was responsible for maintenance of personnel records, general administration of the ZPRA Headquarters (HQ), maintenance of discipline in the force using the Disciplinary Code, drawing a training programme for ZPRA according to the strategic plan and coordinating the recruitment of personnel. This drew a line of recruitment policy of who we recruit how and why, how we draw up what you would call a modern-day military syllabus of what we teach the recruits in the context of our own war that we were pursuing.

Let me comment about women in general. The need to include or rather recruit women was quite appealing because the struggle needed more recruits that would serve as personnel in various departments without necessarily deploying them in the front. I think I have to repeat this, that as we drew the military syllabus of training, it was not to train women and later deploy them into the front but rather for them to receive the training and later occupy various departments within the party and her military wing. We had various departments and those departments needed militarily trained people not an ordinary person.

---

[24]The meeting was held in 1972 in Lusaka, Zambia. It was a conference of militants which sought to strategize the war efforts under the theme, 'The final push.' It clearly spelt out strategies of recruitment, deployment and the front operations among other things. All these military strategies formalized during the conference were bundled together and published as a handbook popularly known as the proxy document. However, the proxy document was later confiscated by the Mugabe-led government, together with disciplinary code, combat diaries, maps, features and operational reports.

One of our policies was to deploy trained military personnel after they internalize party ideology, military strategy and end game vision of why the struggle was waged. It was impossible to recruit women and deploy them in strategic units without training. We also worked on making the forces to improve and manage without basic requirements because we were a guerilla army, while the fourth was to develop the recruit's military and political skills and the right attitude to face up with determination the enemy and challenges that might be encountered.

The training was designed to prepare the recruits to achieve maximum ability within the shortest period and with very limited resources to score successes. This is the reason why we did not have a military training that was different between men and women because our aim was to train a soldier and not to dwell much on differences. We also aimed to develop the female recruit's military and political skills and the right attitude to face the enemy and challenges with determination.

The enemy was going to be able to tame them in their own way and later use them to destroy our leadership and the party together with its military wing. The war council which was known as the revolutionary council agreed to recruit women who were girls as from thirteen years. At that moment, the plan had been to recruit, train them and deploy them to strategic departments like intelligence, and secretarial positions among other things. ZPRA had no plans to deploy women to the front even if our training was tough and never discriminated on the basis of gender. At the helm of all this, I was among the few who were selected to instruct the new recruits of girls according to the military training scheme that we had developed with other comrades in the war council.

In 1975, a group of nine women was recruited. When they finally came to Mwembeshi in Zambia, the war council agreed that it was a manageable number of female recruits. Like I said we never trained women [differently from] men. Where it meant beating them up, being rough and exercising our military powers so that they understand the nature of the training, we did all that.

The emphasis on our training was that it was non-discriminatory and never entertained any stereotypes that you are a man or a woman and that we prefer to recruit this particular tribe because they are stronger than the other. This was not the case; women recruits were trained like men and we saw no distinction. To improve physical fitness, they all ran very early in the morning. I have to be frank with you that they faced difficulties sometimes. Some ran with average speed while others lagged behind.

Female recruits were introduced to some trainings that emphasized the general soldier behavior, military gear and inspection. On this we emphasized on the protocol, time management, resilience and respect. We also introduced them to combat tactics and that covered things like ground and terrain usage, individual camouflage, target identification, distance estimation and individual stalking. Such an exercise was done during the day and night to give an appreciation of both situations. This was coupled with emphasis on teamwork and we started at section level. At that stage the soldiers were taught combat orders and models, stalking, reconnaissance, section battle drills, raids and withdrawal, as well as ambushes and withdrawal.

We made sure that our training was not child's play. We took them through judo for self-defense and under that we emphasized on falls or landing, blockings, throws and kicks, which we wanted to be vicious. There were also drills on close combat such as the bayonet charge, blockings, butting and use of jungle knives. Regarding, obstacle crossing, they were taken through jumping, crawling, negotiating, avoiding through obstacles, jungle lane. To ensure endurance they ran with 20kg kits on their backs. We also took them on topography exercises where they had to master map reading, inland navigation (day and night), use of compass and sketching. Women did all that. I remember when we got attacked at Mgagao, most female recruits managed to come out from the obstacle because of the hard training they had received. I saw them crawl, running, and escaping the violent clash that was an attack on us by ZANLA and Chinese instructors.[25] I was their instructor who commanded them outside the violent clash that was directed to us by our ZANLA counterparts and the Chinese. I was very impressed to see them in action fighting, a sign that made us recommend recruitment of more female combatants to the war council as we had seen that it was feasible to train them effectively.

During the training some would come to me complaining of exhaustion, we would listen to them but encourage them to continue nonetheless. Female recruits were a pleasure to train as they would go beyond the expected in terms of the assignment. During physical training we would make war cries, and chant slogans, and you would imagine if such chants and slogans are also recited by females, it gives them morale.

In my later years of working with female recruits I was assigned to supervise other training camps to best see how they are training as the war intensified. I was happy to see female combatants training others. Those that we had trained in Mwembeshi and Mgagao became instructors to recruits of other females and some men in other camps. Positions with the ZPRA rank and file, intelligence, administration among other things came about because we knew them and never doubted their training. The reason why Smith later targeted female recruits when he bombed them in Mkushi was the fact that he knew that we trained them in the same order we trained their male counterparts hence they posed as more dangerous more than men in the field of intelligence and counter intelligence. If women were of no value, Smith would have bombed camps like Freedom Camps which had refugees, but [he] targeted an all-female training camp to deter them from receiving training.

I end by saying our training was not treated in isolation on the basis that she is a woman or these are men. We all gave them similar training!

---

[25] Also refer to the interview by Grace Mutshatshi, Bvundzai Tawona and Stanford Moyo.